IMAGES
of America

PHILADELPHIA
ORGANIZED CRIME IN
THE 1920s AND 1930s

ON THE COVER: Here, 1st Sgt. Thomas F. Martin and an unidentified officer, both of the Pennsylvania State Police, raid a storage shed used to house illegal liquor during Prohibition. This photograph dates from around 1923. The Pennsylvania State Police performed urban and rural sweeps to enforce Prohibition, a national law that inadvertently spurred the growth of organized crime in the 1920s and 1930s. The state police also patrolled waterways; in 1931, state troopers seized a boat on the Delaware River, just south of Morrisville, Pennsylvania, loaded with $100,000 worth of bootleg liquor. Three of the five crew members were from Philadelphia, and authorities believed the liquor had been consigned for Trenton, New Jersey, a city 30 miles north of Philadelphia. (Pennsylvania State Police Museum.)

IMAGES
of America

PHILADELPHIA
ORGANIZED CRIME IN
THE 1920S AND 1930S

Anne Margaret Anderson
and John J. Binder

ARCADIA
PUBLISHING

Published by Arcadia Publishing
Charleston, South Carolina

Printed in the United States of America

Library of Congress Control Number: 2013946694

For all general information, please contact Arcadia Publishing:
Telephone 843-853-2070
Fax 843-853-0044
E-mail sales@arcadiapublishing.com
For customer service and orders:
Toll-Free 1-888-313-2665

Visit us on the Internet at www.arcadiapublishing.com

Annie dedicates this book to her family,
for encouraging her to tell these stories.

John dedicates this book to his wife, Linda,
who enables this, the most interesting of his hobbies.

CONTENTS

ACKNOWLEDGMENTS

As historians, we are indebted to the librarians, researchers, and technicians who have organized and digitized so many pieces of Philadelphia history. Specifically, archivists like John Pettit, David Baugh, Megan Good, and Aurora Deshauteurs make doing history in the City of Brotherly Love an adventure and a pleasure. Research trips to Temple University's Special Collections Research Center, the Philadelphia City Archives, the Independence Seaport Museum, and the Philadelphia Free Library proved, without fail, surprising and enlightening. Early on in this book's gestation, Philadelphia historian Celeste Morello provided nuanced insights and helpful leads. Thomas Memmi at the Pennsylvania State Police Museum was incredibly generous with his time and resources. His grandfather Thomas F. Martin graces the cover of this book. Our editor, Abby Henry, and our publisher, Rebekah Collinsworth, skillfully guided this project from proposal to completion. Annie is indebted to her exceptionally talented and inspiring colleagues at Eastern State Penitentiary, especially Erica Harman and Sean Kelley for their hustle and support, Fran Dolan for the gift of this book, and Lauren Zalut for her friendship. This book would be unimaginable without the loving, encouraging support of Annie's kith and kin, from Chicago to Boston to Philadelphia. She is especially grateful to her extraordinary family: her lovely parents, Mary and Don; her brilliant sisters, Candice and Tina; and to those who have inspired and sustained her for years, even decades: Steven, Dae, Aunt Joan, Uncle Clar, and Nick. Lastly, Annie is endlessly thankful to Liz, for being there and bearing witness.

INTRODUCTION

The years between the world wars provide American historians with numerous research opportunities. The Roaring Twenties and the Turbulent Thirties embody great possibilities as well as frustrations. In narratives of this era, the themes of disruption and change usually appear as persistent threads. As this book will show, it is hard to imagine what cultural symbol better represents the idea of upheaval than the criminal, that law-breaking, norm-shattering individual. As historian Kristofer Allerfeldt has observed, it is almost unimaginable that an account of modern America would not deal with crime, because crime and criminals make as good a definition of the modern United States as any other. Several classic American motifs—from the law-enforcing Western sheriff to the urban gangster to the hard-boiled detective—all deal with crime. This point about the United States—that crime is an essential character trait of both its personality and popular culture—could not be any truer of Philadelphia in the interwar era.

And yet, compared to New York and Chicago, not much has been written about organized crime in Philadelphia in this era. Nearly 30 years ago, crime historian Mark Haller begged the question "Who can name a Philadelphia bootlegger?" The same question could be asked today of any Philadelphia criminal from this time period. This book aims to answer these questions and to tell many of those forgotten or untold stories. As seen in the photographs and captions that follow, there was widespread organized crime in Philadelphia, and in many ways, it shaped the character of the city.

As *Collier's* magazine noted in 1928, in the midst of a major grand jury investigation into bootlegging and its attendant gang violence, "Lawlessness was the price Philadelphia had to pay for what it wanted to drink." Indeed, the disregard for Prohibition laws in Philadelphia may have created a general disregard for *all* laws. Philadelphia's corrupt culture—in which politicians and police could be bought and sold to protect common crooks and criminal dynasties—shaded how its citizens viewed lawbreakers. Additionally, Philadelphia mobsters kept a lower profile than their Chicago and New York counterparts, which in turn kept Philadelphia's underworld hidden from many Quaker City citizens. Still, the dearth of accessible information on Philadelphia organized crime in the 1920s and 1930s continues to affect which stories are told and which individuals and incidents remain out of sight and out of mind.

Organized criminal groups were plentiful in Philadelphia in the interwar era. But what does it mean to be organized? This book is not solely about Philadelphia's bootlegging gangs and the later criminal groups they spawned, although some of the characters herein belonged to both. It is about racketeers, dope peddlers, gamblers, and insurance schemers. We take a fairly liberal approach to the word "organized." On the whole, the individuals we showcase worked outside the law, as part of a family, ring, or band of criminals.

Chapter One looks at the police, politicians, and power brokers who oversaw—and in some cases, were taken in by—organized crime in the 1920s and 1930s. Chapter Two uncovers the worlds of two of the biggest bootleggers of the era: Max "Boo Boo" Hoff and Mickey Duffy. Gangster alliances and rivalries are revealed in Chapter Three, the title of which, "Bloody Angles," is taken from a particular street corner in South Philadelphia that saw a tremendous amount of violence. Chapter Four investigates Harry "Nig Rosen" Stromberg's mob, an organization that spanned decades and stretched over several East Coast cities. Lastly, Chapter Five examines a poison-for-profit arsenic ring, a sensational, scandalous story made even more so by the Philadelphia press.

This book is a history of a few select groups of people whose photographs were saved over the years. Because it is a pictorial history, we have had to work with what the historical record has preserved in photographic form. Though we found traces of well-known figures in paper records, we were unable to locate photographs of bigger crime kingpins like Salvatore Sabella or John Scopoletti. Meanwhile, we found a number of fascinating images of lower-ranking individuals. In some cases, we were stymied by the lack of information in the historic record. In other cases, we made connections among groups and individuals that we could not have imagined, connections that enriched the book and helped us tell a more cohesive story. The complex project of telling these stories in a visual manner is a nice mirror onto the larger project of "doing history," with all of its limits and possibilities. For the most part, we have used the records of those who enforced laws and supervised criminals. This represents more of a "top-down" version of history. Still, by using official records, as well as newspapers, books, and scholarly articles, we can learn a lot about those who were under the supervision of law enforcement—their habits, their nicknames, their friends and family, and more.

We hope that this book provides insights into the criminal worlds that gave shape to the city in this time period. This history fits into the much larger story of Philadelphia, the East Coast, and the United States in this era, and we recognize that there is still much more to be said about the places and individuals herein. We would love to hear from our readers who have questions or comments. We can be reached at PhiladelphiaOrganizedCrime@gmail.com.

One

CORRUPT AND CONTENTED
POLICE, POLITICIANS,
AND POWER BROKERS

Using 1930 census data, this map shows Philadelphia's ward boundaries and state representatives. Congressman Benjamin Golder of Philadelphia's Fourth District served as Al Capone's lawyer while the Chicago gangster was incarcerated in Philadelphia from late 1929 to early 1930. Golder also provided legal representation to the Franklin Mortgage & Investment Co., one of the biggest bootlegging ventures in Philadelphia, overseen by Capone ally Max "Boo Boo" Hoff. (Philadelphia City Archives.)

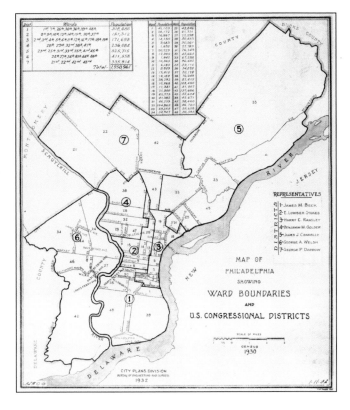

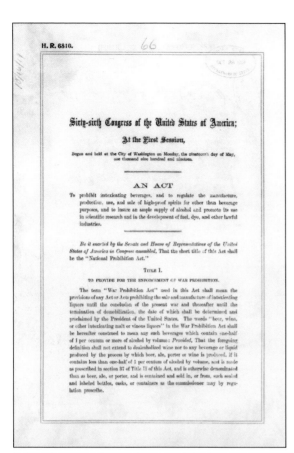

The National Prohibition Act (left), also known as the Volstead Act, regulated the manufacture, use, and sale of intoxicating beverages. Philadelphia became known as an "open town" in this era—one that allowed and encouraged its citizens to ignore the Prohibition laws. Indeed, Prohibition ushered in a new era of illegal enterprises in the City of Brotherly Love, as this saying among businessmen in 1920s Philadelphia demonstrates: "He used to go to New York on business. Since Volstead came, he goes to Philadelphia." Many Philadelphia speakeasies and hotels offering guests liquor were located downtown (below), between city hall and Washington Square. (Left, National Archives and Records Administration; below, Philadelphia City Archives.)

KEY
— PARKING ONE HOUR 9.30 A.M. TO 5 P.M.
~~~~ PARKING UNLIMITED 6.30 P.M. TO 3 A.M.
    NO PARKING AT ANY TIME ON UNSHADED STREETS

BETWEEN SPRING GARDEN AND SOUTH STREETS
AND SCHUYLKILL AND DELAWARE RIVERS NO
PARKING AT ANY TIME ON ANY STREET OF
20 FEET OR LESS FROM CURB TO CURB.

NO PARKING ON ANY HIGHWAY IN THE CITY
BETWEEN 3 A.M. AND SUNRISE.

Nicknamed "Old Gimlet Eyes" and "the Fighting Quaker," Smedley Butler (right) was Philadelphia's director of public safety—the equivalent of police commissioner—from 1924 to 1925. Overseeing the police and fire departments, Butler brought his military background to bear on his public service. According to the *Literary Digest*, "In inviting him to take charge of their police system, the Philadelphia authorities made a gesture of despair and grasped at a desperate remedy." Other critics noted that Butler was "out of his element" in trying to govern a vice-ridden city. Despite—or perhaps because of—his knack for ruffling feathers, Butler produced results. Over the course of his first year in Philadelphia, police closed 2,566 speakeasies, in contrast with just 220 the previous year. In the first four months of 1924, Philadelphia police made 39,000 arrests, keeping police superintendent William Mills's office (below) buzzing. (Right, Library of Congress; below, Philadelphia City Archives.)

Smedley Butler took the oath of office as director of public safety in his Marine uniform, but 30 minutes later, he reappeared in a uniform he had designed himself: a blue getup with gold trim and an ostentatious red-lined cape. He immediately got to work, meeting with police inspectors and ordering a 48-hour cleanup of all of Philadelphia's 42 districts. Butler quickly realized that the city's 48 voting wards aligned almost identically to the 42 police districts. In an effort to reduce the strong grasp that ward bosses had on the police, he reduced the number of police districts to 22. Butler claimed that this move not only had the potential to curb corruption, but it also freed up more officers to police the streets, by foot, car, or patrol wagon (below). (Left, Library of Congress; below, Philadelphia City Archives.)

Philadelphia employed 5,000 police officers in the mid-1920s, many of them taking bribes from bootleggers, prostitution houses, and other illegal entities. In turn, these police officers contributed to corrupt ward politicians who handpicked police captains and provided job protection. One policeman estimated that politicians took one day's pay per month from each of the 7,000 men employed as police and firefighters. Above, two policemen were photographed on the Benjamin Franklin Parkway. Auguste Rodin's famous sculpture *The Thinker* can be seen just above the vehicle's windshield. (Philadelphia City Archives.)

Smedley Butler established an elite force of 250 policemen, nicknamed "Unit No. 1," which handled all vice raids in the city. He established a culture of enforcement so strict that, as *Collier's* magazine noted, "To be an enemy of Butler meant, in effect, to be a friend of crooks, bootleggers and out-and-out criminals from whom Philadelphia has suffered a reign of terror." In the 1920s, law enforcement officials increasingly used automobiles like the one above to fight crime. (Philadelphia City Archives.)

CAFÉ

100% CAFÉ

BONE DRY IN JUNE!
PREPARE NOW!
Lay in a Stock of our
WHISKEY at the **OLD PRICE**
Before the **NEW TAX** is added.

PROHIBITION SURE!
with another Tax due any day
BE WISE & BUY NOW!
To-Morrow may be too late!
Our Whiskey at $6⁰⁰ per gal Unsurpassed

Declaring "Prohibition Sure!" this café (above) advised its patrons to stock up on whiskey before Prohibition set in. Shortly after Prohibition went into effect in 1919, barrels of alcoholic contraband, most likely beer, were dumped into a body of water. As time went on and it became clear that the government could not legislate morality and that the attempt to do so had extreme negative effects, some of the staunchest "dry" politicians became vocal opponents of Prohibition. (Both, John Binder Collection.)

When Mayor Freeland Kendrick (left, shaking hands with boxer Jack Dempsey) was sworn into office on January 7, 1924, Smedley Butler assumed his role as director of public safety. While running for mayor, Kendrick had pleaded with Pres. Calvin Coolidge to release Butler from the Marine Corps to help Philadelphia battle its crime problem. "I know of no man big enough for this task except General Butler," Kendrick said. "Frankly, Mr. President, if the request is denied, I do not know where to run to secure a man who will be able to cope with this dangerous and unusual situation." Kendrick's initial enthusiasm about Butler faded once the hard-line Marine took office. Butler immediately clashed with Kendrick (below left) and the Republican political machine, including South Philadelphia ward boss William Vare (below right). (Both, Library of Congress.)

15

Despite its Quaker heritage and nickname as the City of Brotherly Love, Prohibition-era Philadelphia was referred to as the following: "the worst machine-ridden city of first rank in the country," "one of the wickedest cities in the United States," and "corrupt and contented." Republican political boss William Vare won a contentious election for a US Senate seat in 1926, though the Senate refused to seat Vare because of evidence of election fraud. (Library of Congress.)

Gifford Pinchot, governor of Pennsylvania from 1923 to 1927 and again from 1931 to 1935, opposed William Vare in the race for US Senate in the fall of 1926. When Vare came out victorious, Pinchot claimed that Vare "partly bought and partly stole" the election. Furious after his Senate loss, Pinchot argued that respectable Pennsylvanians were "willing to shut their eyes and make common cause with gangsters, vote thieves, dive keepers, criminals and harlots." (Library of Congress.)

J. Hampton Moore (above) served as mayor of Philadelphia from 1920 to 1924 and again from 1932 to 1936. Just before Moore was replaced by Freeland Kendrick, he called Kendrick's plan to bring Smedley Butler on as Philadelphia's director of public safety "a spectacular misuse of the White House" and claimed that the city's crime problem could be solved by simply increasing the police force. Like many Philadelphia mayors of this era, Moore was no stranger to political fireworks, including clashes with police heads. When the Philadelphia Criminal Justice Association tasked Moore with either supporting or removing Director of Public Safety Kern Dodge (below), he chose the latter action. Dodge in turn charged Moore with playing a political power game. As the *New York Times* observed, "Harmony between a Quaker City Mayor and his Director of Public Safety is one of those goals seldom achieved." (Both, Library of Congress.)

THE BELLEVUE - STRATFORD, PHILADELPHIA,

In some of his final bids to enforce Prohibition in Philadelphia, Smedley Butler sought to revoke the dance license held by the Bellevue-Stratford Hotel (left) and attempted to padlock the Ritz-Carlton Hotel's doors. Within a month of Prohibition officers raiding a formal ball at the Ritz-Carlton and seizing bottles of wine and champagne, the hotel remained open and Butler had left Philadelphia for good. In going after hotel proprietors, Butler attempted to "teach these big fellows that they must obey the law as well as the little fellows." As police records reveal (below), the city's vice squad busted the lowly, such as saloons, barbershops, candy stores, and the like, as well as the swanky, including the Ritz-Carlton Hotel. Later on in the 1920s, "Prohibition's Mr. Big," Mickey Duffy, a bootlegger and racketeer, lived in a suite at the Ritz-Carlton. (Left, Library of Congress; below, Philadelphia City Archives.)

374		24	Saloon, Frankford ave, & Willard St.	"
375		36	Barber Shop, Lycoming & Fairhill St.	"
376	P	36	Saloon 6th & Luzerne Sts.	"
377	P	31	Candy Store, 27th & Fletcher Sts	"
378	P	42	51st & Lancaster ave. Empty house, Still	.
379	P	28	1825 Diamond St.	Dis. House
380	P	18	Marshall St. above Dauphin St.	Liquor
381	P	5	Ritz Carlton Hotel (Grill)	"
382	P	1	2523 Christian St.	"
383	P	30	Saloon, Front & Cambria St.	"
384	P.	24	S. W. cor. Allegheny & Arbor St. (Saloon)	"

Gen. Smedley Butler, Philadelphia's director of public safety from 1924 to 1925, smashes a barrel of beer with a pickax after a raid (right). Below, another Prohibition enforcer smashes a barrel, letting loose a geyser of illicit alcohol. (Right, Library of Congress; below, John Binder Collection.)

A well-known speakeasy, Club Madrid (seen at center of the photograph) entertained its share of high-powered guests, including Republican magistrate Edward Carney, who investigated liquor law violators by day while patronizing them at night. Just off Broad Street in Center City Philadelphia, Club Madrid was the site of one of Smedley Butler's raids during his tenure as director of public safety. (Philadelphia City Archives.)

In this typical Prohibition-era raid, the authorities smashed bottles and barrels in front of curious, and possibly thirsty, onlookers. Such photographs gave an air of legitimacy to Prohibition enforcement, but the reality of the dry era was quite different, with many police officers and Prohibition agents taking bribes so that the bootleggers and bar owners could operate unhindered. Some of the enforcers actually changed sides and became bootleggers after learning the ins and outs of the business. (John Binder Collection.)

Just a handful of days into Smedley Butler's tenure as director of public safety, he announced that 973 saloons had closed their doors. The city's bootleggers and speakeasies quickly got a taste of Butler's "pounce policy," a strategy that entailed sudden and repeated raids. While Butler took his job very seriously, others in power thought less highly of Prohibition and its enforcement. Upon leaving Philadelphia at the end of 1925, Butler quipped, "I have been fighting in a battle where the head of the show was disloyal and everything was crooked." Of Gen. William Temcumseh Sherman's famous phrase "war is hell," Butler told reporters, "Sherman was right about war, but he was never head of police in Philadelphia." (John Binder Collection.)

Philadelphia's location at the confluence of the Delaware and Schuylkill Rivers, just inland from the Atlantic Ocean, enabled shipments of bootleg alcohol via land and sea. This 1930s poster advertised Philadelphia as a bustling port city accessible to both ships and trucks. (Library of Congress.)

The US Coast Guard patrolled the waterways along the Eastern Seaboard, keeping an eye out for rumrunners, boats used to convey bootleg liquor. Here, a rumrunner chaser is inspected at the Navy Yard in Washington, DC. Philadelphia ports accommodated several famous rumrunners, including Bill McCoy and Johnny Campbell. (Library of Congress.)

Atlantic City, New Jersey, about 60 miles from Philadelphia, was considered neutral territory for organized criminals. The seaside town hosted a "peace summit" of gangsters at the President Hotel in May 1929. After the summit, on his journey back to Chicago, Al Capone was arrested in Philadelphia and imprisoned there for 10 months for carrying a concealed weapon. Philadelphia bootlegger Mickey Duffy, an Atlantic City regular, was assassinated in his beachfront hotel room in 1931. (Library of Congress.)

Lemuel Schofield (left) became the city's director of public safety in the late 1920s, overseeing one of the city's most high-profile arrests of an organized crime figure: that of Al Capone in 1929. Schofield later served as attorney for several bootleggers he once prosecuted, including Mickey Duffy affiliate Herman "Whitey" Cohen as well as members of the infamous Philadelphia arsenic ring. He is pictured here with Solicitor General Francis Biddle (center) and Attorney General Robert Jackson (right). (Library of Congress.)

In February 1930, Lemuel Schofield led a raid on two private suites in the Benjamin Franklin Hotel, where police recovered several bottles of whiskey and gin. "Long ago I served notice on all of the large hotels in Philadelphia," Schofield remarked, "that if they permitted liquor to be brought into the hotels, they could expect trouble. If these violations continue, the raids will continue." (Anne Margaret Anderson.)

In 1932, hotel proprietor Edward Skinner, like many hotel employees of this era, was swept up in Prohibition's wide net. He was incarcerated at Philadelphia's Eastern State Penitentiary for possession and sale of intoxicating liquor. (Eastern State Penitentiary Historic Site.)

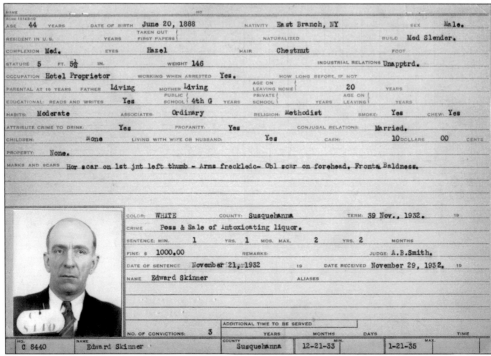

NAME   NO
Acme 13143-10
AGE 44   YEARS   DATE OF BIRTH June 20, 1888   NATIVITY East Branch, NY   SEX   Male.
RESIDENT IN U.S.   YEARS   TAKEN OUT / FIRST PAPERS {   NATURALIZED   BUILD Med Slender.
COMPLEXION Med.   EYES   Hazel   HAIR   Chestnut   FOOT
STATURE 5 FT. 5½ IN.   WEIGHT 146   INDUSTRIAL RELATIONS Unapptrd.
OCCUPATION Hotel Proprietor   WORKING WHEN ARRESTED Yes.   HOW LONG BEFORE, IF NOT
PARENTAL AT 10 YEARS FATHER Living   MOTHER Living   AGE ON LEAVING HOME 20   YEARS
EDUCATIONAL: READS AND WRITES Yes   PUBLIC SCHOOL 4th G YEARS   PRIVATE SCHOOL YEARS   AGE ON LEAVING YEARS
HABITS: Moderate   ASSOCIATES: Ordinary   RELIGION: Methodist   SMOKE: Yes   CHEW: Yes
ATTRIBUTE CRIME TO DRINK: Yes   PROFANITY: Yes   CONJUGAL RELATIONS: Married.
CHILDREN: None   LIVING WITH WIFE OR HUSBAND: Yes   CASH: 10 DOLLARS 00 CENTS
PROPERTY: None.
MARKS AND SCARS Hor scar on 1st jnt left thumb - Arms freckledo- Obl scar on forehead. Fronta Baldness.

COLOR: WHITE   COUNTY: Susquehanna   TERM: 39 Nov., 1932.   19
CRIME Poss & Sale of intoxicating liquor.
SENTENCE: MIN. 1 YRS. 1 MOS. MAX. 2 YRS. 2 MONTHS
FINE: $ 1000.00   REMARKS: JUDGE: A.B.Smith.
DATE OF SENTENCE November 21, 1932   19   DATE RECEIVED November 29, 1932. 19
NAME Edward Skinner   ALIASES

NO. OF CONVICTIONS: 3   ADDITIONAL TIME TO BE SERVED YEARS MONTHS DAYS   TIME
NO. C 8440   NAME Edward Skinner   COUNTY Susquehanna   MIN. 12-21-33   MAX. 1-21-35

19 YEARS	DATE OF BIRTH August 8th,1909	NATIVITY Philadelphia, Pa.			SEX male	

DENT IN U. S. YEARS TAKEN OUT FIRST PAPERS   NATURALIZED   BUILD Medium

PLEXION Dark EYES Dark Green Slate HAIR Dark Chestnut FOOT 10

URE 5 FT. 4 IN. WEIGHT 143 INDUSTRIAL RELATIONS Unapprenticed

PATION Bootlegger WORKING WHEN ARRESTED no HOW LONG BEFORE, IF NOT never worked

NTAL AT 16 YEARS FATHER living MOTHER living AGE ON LEAVING HOME never left YEARS

ATIONAL: READS AND WRITES yes PUBLIC SCHOOL 7 YEARS PRIVATE SCHOOL YEARS AGE ON LEAVING 14 YEARS

RS: Moderate ASSOCIATES: Bad RELIGION: Hebrew SMOKE: yes CHEW: no

IBUTE CRIME TO DRINK: no PROFANITY: yes CONJUGAL RELATIONS: Single

DREN: LIVING WITH WIFE OR HUSBAND: CASH: 5 DOLLARS CE

PERTY: 1 Key; Scar on 1st ph left index finger rear; Small round scar on grow h on lobe of left ear; Scar

KS AND SCARS of Appendix operation on right groin;

COLOR: White COUNTY: Philadelphia TERM: 690 May 1929 19

CRIME Entering with intent to Steal

SENTENCE: MIN. 2 YRS. 6 MOS. MAX. 10 YRS. MONTHS

FINE: $ 1.00 REMARKS: Accomplice C5389 JUDGE: Gordon Jr.

DATE OF SENTENCE May 20-1929 19 DATE RECEIVED May 20-1929 19

NAME Morris Jacobs ALIASES Morris Glimer

Morris Gleaner

See Remarks on Reverse Side

NO. OF CONVICTIONS: 1

ADDITIONAL TIME TO BE SERVED YEARS MONTHS DAYS TIME

O.	NAME	COUNTY	MIN.		MAX.	
C5388	Morris Jacobs	Philadelphia	11-20-31		5-20-39	

Though 19-year-old Morris Jacobs was sentenced to Eastern State Penitentiary for entering with intent to steal, his occupation was listed as "Bootlegger." Jacobs had either admitted this information about himself, or prison authorities had gathered evidence to make this claim. Bootleggers like Jacobs operated within a black market economy in which those flouting one law often broke other laws. A few years prior to Jacobs's arrest, the *Literary Digest* described Pennsylvania as a "bootleggers' Elysium." The magazine diagnosed the entire Keystone State as suffering from a "liquor deluge," with every city as "wet as the Atlantic Ocean." (Eastern State Penitentiary Historic Site.)

Though no evidence ties Michael Joseph Thomas and his accomplice Thomas Michael Magee to organized crime, their Eastern State Penitentiary intake cards point out the underworld to which their crime belonged. The two men robbed a speakeasy in May 1933, just months before Prohibition was repealed. In Prohibition-era Philadelphia, police records acknowledged that 8,000 illegal, unlicensed taverns operated throughout the city. Journalists estimated there were at least 8,000 more "blind tigers," another term for speakeasies, where intoxicants were sold. (Both, Eastern State Penitentiary Historic Site.)

In 1929, when an angry mob of 500 people threw rocks at Philadelphia Prohibition agents following a raid, Pennsylvania State Police troopers intervened and escorted the agents to safety. The agents confiscated 1,600 gallons of wine, 97 quarts of whiskey and gin, 19 barrels of beer, and 130 bottles of beer from hotels and restaurants. A trooper (far left) stands guard outside a shoeshine shop, the site of a raid, in downtown Reading, Pennsylvania. (Pennsylvania State Police Museum.)

A member of the Pennsylvania State Police since 1905, Maj. Lynn G. Adams (front row, left) served as superintendent of the state police from 1920 to 1937 and commissioner of the state police from 1939 to 1943. Adams led a force of fewer than 300 men in making more than 3,000 arrests in liquor cases in 1923 alone. (Pennsylvania State Police Museum.)

With this 1929 press photograph advertising Pennsylvania's new license plates, the state police pointed out the already indelible connection between crime and the automobile. The model displays the license plate as if holding her mug shot booking card. Organized criminals in this era often used cars—for everything from the distribution of illegal alcohol to drive-by shootings. The exploding popularity of cars in the 1920s allowed Americans unprecedented mobility and opportunities to see and do more things—illicit or otherwise—than ever before. Many industrial capitalists, thinking of high profits driven by sober workers, supported Prohibition. Car king Henry Ford referred to the 18th Amendment as "the greatest force for the comfort and prosperity of the U.S." *Time* magazine quickly labeled him as "Prohibition's prime industrial protagonist." (Pennsylvania State Police Museum.)

With organized crime becoming more sophisticated as Prohibition wore on, the Philadelphia Police Department formed a Bandit Division in November 1928. Director of Public Safety Harry C. Davis promised a "relentless war on banditry" to address and prevent holdups, automobile thefts, and similar crimes. Like their criminal counterparts, the 300 policemen in this new division were equipped with "all the bandit-chasing equipment now in the department, including automobiles, motorcycles, shotguns and machine guns," according to the *New York Times*. The Bandit Division was assembled in the wake of the 1928 Special August Grand Jury, convened to investigate bootlegging and the escalating gang violence associated with it. Here, a Philadelphia policeman stands next to a primitive motorcycle, which was little more than a mechanized bicycle. (Philadelphia City Archives.)

Prohibition commissioner Dr. James Doran (pictured) ordered an entire unit of the Internal Revenue Service's intelligence department to Philadelphia in 1928 to aid District Attorney John Monaghan in a grand jury investigation into bootlegging and corruption. Like the order sending Gen. Smedley Butler to Philadelphia in 1924, this was another move on the part of the federal government to help Philadelphia deal with its Prohibition-fueled crime problem. (Library of Congress.)

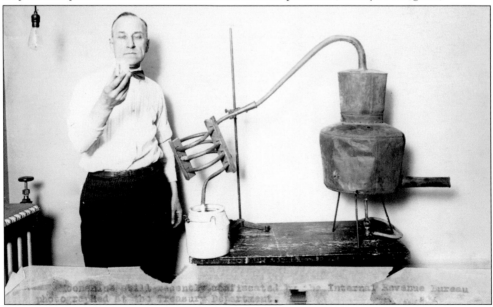

On December 11, 1933, just after Prohibition ended, the US attorney general announced that the entire force of 1,170 federal Prohibition agents would be deputized by the Internal Revenue Service to "prevent bootlegging and other illegal liquor operations," now that liquor was again legalized. Here, an IRS agent examines the contents of a moonshine still. (Library of Congress.)

US assistant attorney general Mabel Walker Willebrandt directed the Internal Revenue Service's intelligence department as it aided in the 1928 Philadelphia grand jury investigation. Willebrandt was one of the first women to attain cabinet-level rank in the US government. Nicknamed "Prohibition Portia," she oversaw all Prohibition cases during her eight years as assistant attorney general. (Library of Congress.)

Pres. Herbert Hoover (front row, third from right) tasked the National Commission on Law Observance and Enforcement (pictured) with assessing law enforcement, particularly Prohibition enforcement. Under George W. Wickersham (front row, second from right), the commission issued just one report before being disbanded. (Library of Congress.)

This Clifford Berryman cartoon pokes fun of George W. Wickersham, commissioner of the short-lived National Commission on Law Observance and Enforcement, also known as the Wickersham Commission. In 1931, its first and only report to Congress stated the vague, obvious truth about the nation's Prohibition-fueled crime problem: something must be done. The *New York World* satirically summarized the report as follows: "Prohibition is an awful flop. We like it. It can't stop what it's meant to stop. We like it. It's left a trail of graft and slime, It's filled our land with vice and crime, It don't prohibit worth a dime, Nevertheless we're for it." (National Archives and Records Administration.)

Smedley Butler's legacy lives on at Philadelphia City Hall, where this bronze plaque hangs in his honor. It reads, "He enforced the law impartially / He defended it courageously / He proved incorruptible." Calling Butler "100 per cent honest," the *Philadelphia Record* wryly observed that Butler's virtuousness was more than Mayor Freeland Kendrick had bargained for. (Anne Margaret Anderson.)

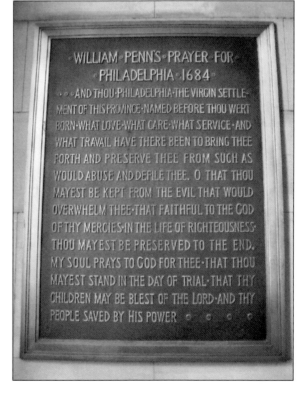

Hanging directly across from Butler's plaque is William Penn's "Prayer for Philadelphia" of 1684. "O that thou mayest be kept from the evil that would overwhelm thee," Penn prayed. Though Butler might have been the kind of protector that Penn had envisioned for his city, Butler's very presence in Philadelphia signaled that the city had indeed been overwhelmed and defiled. (Anne Margaret Anderson.)

Two

THE KING AND MR. BIG
BOOTLEGGING EMPIRES

Philadelphia district attorney John Monaghan labeled Max "Boo Boo" Hoff (pictured) as the "King of the Bootleggers." Hoff's diminutive stature belied his tremendous influence as a boxing promoter, club owner, and proprietor of several industrial alcohol firms that diverted their product to bootleg liquor. (John Binder Collection.)

Max "Boo Boo" Hoff came under investigation during the 1928 Special August Grand Jury, which revealed that hundreds of Philadelphia police officers had received bribes for protecting bootlegging operations and speakeasies. The grand jury discovered that Philadelphia Director of Public Safety George Elliott and several high-ranking police officials were on Hoff's Christmas gift list. Elliott's housekeeper signed for a Christmas package bearing the inscription "Merry Christmas and Happy New Year from Boo Boo Max Hoff and the boys." A spate of gangland killings, including those of club owner Hugh McLoon and bootlegger Daniel O'Leary, prompted the grand jury investigation. District Attorney John Monaghan helped padlock more than 1,000 speakeasies over the course of the investigation, but the grand jury hardly proclaimed victory over liquor law violators. Monaghan estimated that $10 million of liquor racket earnings, deposited in various banks under false names, lined the coffers of Philadelphia bootleggers. (John Binder Collection.)

Max "Boo Boo" Hoff ran a speakeasy out of this castle-like building near Thirteenth and Locust Streets. Called the 21 Club, the nightspot got its name from its address: 1321 Locust Street. A stone's throw from the 21 Club was another Hoff nightspot, the Picadilly Club, which Hoff co-owned with Charles Schwartz and Samuel Lazar. The Picadilly Club came under investigation by the 1928 Special August Grand Jury. While investigating the speakeasies that served illegal liquor, Philadelphia district attorney John Monaghan also set his sights on the places that manufactured the illicit product, boasting, "Not a brewery or distillery is operating now in Philadelphia." Despite Monaghan's claim, the Special August Grand Jury did not shift public opinion on Prohibition or stop bootlegging-related gang violence. A 1928 *Chicago Daily Tribune* headline humorously summed up Philadelphia's regard of liquor laws: "In Philadelphia Prohibition Is Only An Opinion." (Philadelphia City Archives.)

Max "Boo Boo" Hoff's office was located in the Hotel Sylvania (halfway down the block on the right), kitty-corner from his 21 Club. During the 1928 grand jury investigation, Hoff's former chauffeur, Louis Elfman, testified that Hoff had entertained Al Capone at the Sylvania. District Attorney John Monaghan latched onto Elfman's testimony, saying, "I want all Philadelphia to know . . . that Hoff and his gang have brought on Chicago gunmen to threaten and intimidate witnesses who may be called." Despite Monaghan's grandiose rhetoric and Hoff's reputation as a "boss bootlegger," Hoff was never indicted on Prohibition charges. (Philadelphia City Archives.)

This Hotel Sylvania matchbook promised "Cocktail Hour Every Hour," presumably in the post-Prohibition era when serving cocktails was legal again. Nightlife fixture Hugh McLoon used the Sylvania as headquarters for his nightclub and sporting ventures. McLoon, a humpbacked little person who once served as the mascot for the Philadelphia Athletics baseball team, managed prizefighters and operated a speakeasy at Tenth and Cuthbert Streets. He was killed in a drive-by shooting in front of his nightclub in 1928. (Both, Anne Margaret Anderson.)

Max "Boo Boo" Hoff operated the Franklin Mortgage & Investment Co. to manage the revenue from his bootlegging ventures. Today, the Franklin Mortgage & Investment Co. is a contemporary speakeasy in downtown Philadelphia, complete with low lights, strong drinks, and no windows. Inside the bar, a mural by Robert Garey depicts scenes from Prohibition-era Philadelphia. Anchoring the mural, in his trademark boater hat, is Max "Boo Boo" Hoff. (Anne Margaret Anderson.)

On the corner of Walnut and Juniper Streets sat the Bankers Trust Building, which housed the offices of Marks, Weinberg & Co., public accountants whose records were seized by the Special August Grand Jury in 1928. The accounting records, which included nearly every big bootlegging operation in Philadelphia, revealed enormous sums of money paid by bootleggers to police for protection. (Anne Margaret Anderson.)

Field	Value
Name	Alphonsus Capone
Sex	Male
Color	White
Alias	
Crime	Carry Cons Deadly Weapons
Place	Phila
Date	May 14-29
Arrested by	Phila Police
Date	May 14-29
City or Town	Phila
County	Phila
State	Penn.
Sentence	1 Year
Sentence Expires	May 12-1930
Marks and Scars	2 Scars left side of Cheek Cut scar left side of neck Operation 2 Scars left side of leg 2 Scars inside of leg 2 scars under
Associates	Frank Cline 1 Year Phila City Prison
Age	30
Nationality	American
Height	5 10½
Occupation	Real Estate
Weight	248
Birth Place	N.Y.C.
Build	Stout
Residence	7244 Paradise Ave
Complexion	Dark
Education	
Hair	Dark
Single—Married	Married
Eyes	Gray
Nose	
Remarks	
Previous Record	
Prisoner's Signature	Alphonse Capone

Form 83—9-29-27—50,000

B5406

Al Capone spent 10 months in prison in Philadelphia, from May 1929 to March 1930. He was arrested, along with his bodyguard Frank Rio, also known as Frank Cline, for carrying a concealed deadly weapon. The swiftness of Capone's arrest and sentencing—the entire affair took less than 24 hours—caused some to suspect that he had arranged his arrest to avoid the repercussions of the St. Valentine's Day Massacre in Chicago, which had occurred three months earlier. No definitive proof emerged to validate this allegation, and Capone made at least six efforts, via legal action, to free himself from prison in Philadelphia. Capone was incarcerated first in Holmesburg Prison, in the far northeast corner of the city, for three months. He was then transferred to Eastern State Penitentiary, close to downtown Philadelphia, where he remained from August 1929 until March 1930. (Pennsylvania State Police Museum.)

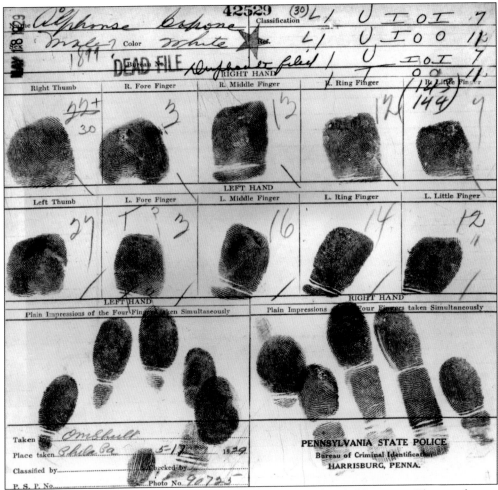

At the time of his arrest in Philadelphia, Al Capone was headed home to Chicago from a gangster "peace summit" in Atlantic City, New Jersey. Prior to this arrest, Capone had never been photographed or fingerprinted (above) by law enforcement officials. When questioned by Philadelphia police, he acknowledged that he was friendly with Max "Boo Boo" Hoff and that there were "connections" between the two city's liquor rings. Hoff visited Capone while the latter was incarcerated at Eastern State Penitentiary. (Pennsylvania State Police Museum.)

Capone appeared thinner and well groomed upon his entrance to Eastern State Penitentiary, where he was transferred from Holmesburg Prison in August 1929. He was imprisoned at Eastern State until his release in March 1930, when he returned to Chicago. A year and a half later, he was back in prison, convicted of tax evasion. Capone died in 1947, not in the 1930s, as this card erroneously indicates. (Pennsylvania State Police Museum.)

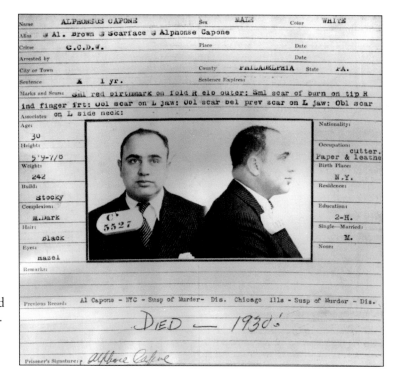

J. Edgar Hoover was appointed director of the Bureau of Investigation in 1924, when he was just 29 years old. His highly publicized war on criminal gangs raised the profile of the bureau, which became the Federal Bureau of Investigation in 1935. In 1931, Hoover personally distributed copies of Al Capone's criminal record to the police departments in Chicago, Miami, and Philadelphia; the Pennsylvania State Police; and Philadelphia's Holmesburg Prison. (Library of Congress.)

3	P	39	3028 n. 21st St. Saloon	"
4	P	6	Turkish Bath House 10th & Cuch Sts.	Immoral Practices
5		21	419 So. 40th St.	Liquor
6		34	1637 Federal St. Pool Room	" & gambling
7	P	7	231 Brown St.	gambling
8	P	24	Cambria, bet. Jasper & Kensington, C lub.	"
9	P	16	Drug Store, 44th & Stiles Sts.	Liquor
0	P	12	1408 n. Marshall St.	"
1	P	7	820 New Market St.	"
2	P	12	1954-55-63 n. Alder St	" & Bawdy House
3	P	26	2915 n. Hasley St.	"

Saloons, bathhouses, poolrooms, and private residencies were the scenes of Philadelphia police vice raids for a variety of offenses: liquor use, gambling, keeping or patronizing a bawdy house, and the nebulous "immoral practices" (above). The area just north of downtown Philadelphia was nicknamed the "Tenderloin" and known for its brothels, vaudeville shows, and booze. Centered around Vine Street in Chinatown, the Tenderloin's red-light influence stretched north to Callowhill Street, south to Race Street, east to Sixth Street, and west to Thirteenth Street. The Turkish Bath House, located at Tenth and Arch Streets, sat at the southern outskirts of the Tenderloin. Philadelphia police vice officers raided the Pekin Café, owned by Mickey Duffy, and recorded the bust in a 1924 logbook (below). (Both, Philadelphia City Archives.)

99		3	Kick & Water Sts.	Liquor
100		23	1306 n. 16th St.	"
101		38	6119 Pine St.	"
102		29	5509 Haverford ave	"
103		12	Pekin Cafe & others	"
104		25	1506-09-11 S. 2nd St.	"
105		4	112 Vine St. cigar store	"
106		11	539 E. Girard ave.	"

EASTERN STATE PENITENTIARY, PA.

Identification Record.

COMMITMENT NAME: JOHN MURPHY, @ MICHAEL DUFFY, @ MIKE DUFFY.   COLOR: White
ALIASES: Michael Duffy,- @ Michael Joseph Duffy, (R.N.)   SEX: Male
                Frank Anderson,- @ George McEwen,- @ Michael Duff,- @ Arnold.
SENTENCED: 5-29-19   FROM: PHILADELPHIA COUNTY
TERM: 2 Years & 11 Months to 3 Years.   CRIME: A. & B. to KILL.
AGE: 30   (9-8-88)   NATIVITY: Philadelphia, Pa.

BERTILLON MEASUREMENTS.

19.3   15.1   11.8   26.5   46.0   72.2   8.8   6.3   71.0   92.2   13.5   5' 7¾   156

HEIGHT
5 ft. 7¾ in.

WEIGHT
156 lbs.

BUILD
Medium

COMPLEXION
Fair

HAIR
Blonde

EYES
Blue

MARKS and SCARS: I* Scr 1 obl wrist frt;   Ft scr 1 obl 3rd jnt index rear;
       II * Scr abcess 2 bel fold elbow inner;
           Scr abcess 9 bel fold elbow outer;
           2 scrs ea 1 vert, & scr 1½ obl @ 1 abv 1st fold mid finger front;
           Ragged scar 2 vert 1st jnt mid finger rear;
           First joint middle finger broken & deformed;
           Third joint little finger deformed.
      III * Scr 1½ hor at & abv tail right eyebrow;
           Scr 2 hor at & abv right eyebrow, 2½ from M. L.;
           Fresh scar 4½ obl on top of head in hair; 2 from M. L.;
           Hair thin on top.

Blond-haired, blue-eyed Mickey Duffy was dubbed "Prohibition's Mr. Big" in 1920s Philadelphia. Born William Michael Cusick to Polish parents, he amassed an array of Irish aliases and Jewish allies during his bootlegging career. Duffy owned several breweries in New Jersey, coordinating shipments into Philadelphia via his Camden headquarters. He also owned several nightclubs and oversaw a gambling syndicate. When not staying at his suite in the lush Ritz-Carlton Hotel downtown, Duffy lived in a mansion in the wealthy Overbrook section of Philadelphia. Fellow club owner William Weiss—who, like Duffy, met a violent, untimely death—was his neighbor there. Duffy survived a several-year stint at Eastern State Penitentiary in the early 1920s and a drive-by shooting attempt on his life in 1927 before being slain in his hotel room in Atlantic City in August 1931. His murder was never solved. (Special Collections Research Center, Temple University Libraries.)

Bootlegging rivals made an attempt on Mickey Duffy's life in 1927 outside of this building on Chestnut Street (above), which housed the Duffy-owned Cadix nightclub. By 1931, the year of his death, Duffy oversaw an extremely divided bootlegging operation. One of Duffy's underlings, Samuel E. Grossman (below), was suspected of plotting his boss's murder. Just months after Duffy was killed, Grossman and Albert Skale were gunned down at the Jewish Social Club, an underworld hangout. Though Grossman and Skale's murders were never solved, it was thought that they were killed by fellow Duffy associates Hyman "Little Krissie" Kriss and Eddie Regan. Though Regan was slain soon after, Kriss enjoyed a sustained career as a gangster, achieving a high rank in the "Nig Rosen" mob into the 1950s. (Above, Anne Margaret Anderson; below, John Binder Collection.)

A top killer in New York gangland, Frankie Carbo was thought to be the gunman behind Mickey Duffy's murder. Police arrested Carbo for the slaying, but evidence was sparse, and he was released. Boxing promoter Mugsy Taylor, who visited Al Capone at Eastern State Penitentiary, claimed to be cozy with Carbo and a number of underworld figures. (John Binder Collection.)

Brothers Francis (far left) and Harry Bailey (far right) flank the other members of their bootlegging gang: (from left to right) Louis "Fats" Barrish, Petey Ford, George "Skinny" Barrow, and Robert Mais. The Baileys, Ford, and Barrish were thought to be behind the 1927 attempted assassination of liquor king Mickey Duffy, with whom they were at odds over bootlegging turf. The media speculated that Max "Boo Boo" Hoff ordered the Bailey gang to kill Duffy, but the historic record shows that Duffy and Hoff—two of the biggest bootleg barons in Philadelphia in this era—coexisted amicably. Petey Ford and Francis Bailey were also held for questioning in the kidnapping of nightlife figure and racketeer William Weiss in 1934. (Philadelphia City Archives.)

Beatrice Dardou	B	11.2.27	Albert Burney		2/28/28	Discharged at court
William Pratt	B	11.2.27	Harry Ford		11/1/27	Discharged by court
Leo Mueller		11.2.27	Commit & Retain		11/4/27	18 Mos C P
Louis Barrish		11.9.27	Thomas Kennedy		11/30/28	E P for Life
Robert Mais		11.9.27	" "		12/31/28	Discharged by court
John J. Feenane		11.22.27	Francis Thomas		3/7/28	2 to 4 Years E P
Francesco Vergora		11.7.27	Manslaughter		11/17/27	Discharged by court
Castell Ebo	B	11.23.27	Raymond Ebo		3/20/28	2½ to 5 Years L P
Willie James	B	11.23.27	George Green		3/2/28	E P for Life
Solomon Kimmelblatt		11.23.27	Esther Kimmelblatt		11/25/27	Discharged by court

Louis "Fats" Barrish and Robert Mais were arrested for the murder of Thomas Kennedy in 1927. Mais was discharged by the court, but Barrish garnered a life sentence to Eastern State Penitentiary. Barrish and fellow inmate Max "Chinkie" Rothman survived a knife fight in the prison yard, and Rothman went on to achieve a high rank in the "Nig Rosen" mob. (Philadelphia City Archives.)

NAME   NO.

FORM P-1 3-6-43 2M

AGE 27 YEARS   DATE OF BIRTH 12-15-07   NATIVITY Phila. Pa.   SEX Male

RESIDENT IN U. S.   YEARS   DATE AND PLACE OF FIRST PAPERS   DATE AND PLACE OF NATURALIZATION

COMPLEXION Ruddy   EYES Dk. Chestnut   HAIR Dk. Red   FOOT   BUILD Med. Slender

STATURE 5 FT. 8 3/8 IN.   WEIGHT 139   INDUSTRIAL RELATIONS Unapprd

OCCUPATION Huckster   WORKING WHEN ARRESTED Yes   HOW LONG BEFORE, IF NOT

PARENTAL AT 16 YEARS   FATHER Living   MOTHER Living   AGE ON LEAVING HOME Never Left   YEARS

EDUCATIONAL: READS AND WRITES Yes   SCHOOL, PUBLIC OR PAROCHIAL 6Gr. YEARS   PRIVATE SCHOOL YEARS   COLLEGE YEARS   AGE ON LEAVING HOME YEARS

HABITS: Moderate   ASSOCIATES: Ordinary   RELIGION: Catholic   SMOKE: Yes   CHEW: No

ATTRIBUTE CRIME TO DRINK: No   PROFANITY: Yes   CONJUGAL RELATIONS: Single

CHILDREN: None   LIVING WITH WIFE OR HUSBAND: CASH: One   DOLLARS 41¢ CENTS

PROPERTY: None

MARKS AND SCARS Obl. scar on bridge of nose; Dimple in chin;

BRIEF HISTORY OF CRIME: Defd assissted in hiding of Wm Weiss(Kidnapped)

COLOR: White   COUNTY: Bucks   TERM: 36 & 50 Feb.& May 1935

CRIME Accessory after the fact of Murder; Secretion of a Kidnapped Person;   JUDGE: Boyer

SENTENCE: MIN. 4 YRS. 0 MOS.   MAX: 8 YRS. 0 MOS.   FINE: $1.00

Sentence on Bill # 36 Suspended

REMARKS Accomp. C-5025;C573 9;C8825;C-83 59;D-498;/Walter Lagenza& Robt Mais;Electrocuted

DATE OF SENTENCE 5-22-35 to begin 2-5-35 19   DATE RECEIVED 5-27-35 19

NAME Joseph James Coffey   ALIASES

EASTERN STATE PENITENTIARY, PA
D-607
5-27-35

NO. OF CONVICTIONS: ADDITIONAL TIME TO BE SERVED   YEARS   MONTHS   DAYS   TIME

NO. D-607   NAME Joseph James Coffey   COUNTY Bucks   MIN. 2-5-39   MAX. 2-5-43

Joseph James Coffey, along with Martin Farrell and other members of Robert Mais's gang, killed nightclub owner and racketeer William Weiss and dumped his body in a creek northeast of Philadelphia. Coffey had allegedly stolen the automobile in which the kidnapped Weiss was transported. Newspapers linked Weiss to fellow liquor racketeer Max "Boo Boo" Hoff, reporting that Hoff was the Mais gang's original kidnapping target. (Eastern State Penitentiary Historic Site.)

| 12143-10 26 | YEARS | DATE OF BIRTH | December 22, 1906 | NATIVITY | Phila., Pa. | | | SEX | Male. |

			NO.				

DENT IN U.S.   YEARS   TAKEN OUT FIRST PAPERS   NATURALIZED   BUILD Med.

PLEXION Med Fair   EYES Hazel   HAIR Light Chestnut   FOOT

TURE 5 FT. 8½ IN.   WEIGHT 158   INDUSTRIAL RELATIONS Apptd.

UPATION Fireman   WORKING WHEN ARRESTED Yes.   HOW LONG BEFORE, IF NOT

ENTAL AT 16 YEARS FATHER Living   MOTHER Living   AGE ON LEAVING HOME 16 YEARS

CATIONAL: READS AND WRITES Yes   PUBLIC SCHOOL 6th G YEARS   PRIVATE SCHOOL YEARS   AGE ON LEAVING YEARS

TS: Occ Intemp   ASSOCIATES: Ordinary   RELIGION: Catholic   SMOKE: Yes   CHEW: Yes

RIBUTE CRIME TO DRINK: No   PROFANITY: Yes   CONJUGAL RELATIONS: Married.

DREN: None   LIVING WITH WIFE OR HUSBAND: Yes   CASH: None. DOLLARS   CEN

PERTY: None.

KS AND SCARS Tat red and blue Anchor surmtg Pennant with USN in print - below fold left elbow. Tat female in tights below fold right elbow.

COLOR: WHITE   COUNTY: Delaware   TERM: 193 June, 1932. 19

CRIME Robbery, Larceny of auto, etc.

SENTENCE: MIN. 6 YRS. 6 MOS. MAX. 13 YRS. 0 MONTHS

FINE: $ 200.00 & Costs.   REMARKS: JUDGE Arird.

DATE OF SENTENCE October 14, 1932 19   DATE RECEIVED October 22, 1932. 19

NAME Martin Farrell   ALIASES Martin Edmond Farrell - Smith. Egan - Thomas Carr.

ADDITIONAL TIME TO BE SERVED

NO. OF CONVICTIONS: YEARS   MONTHS   DAYS   TIME

NO. C 8359	NAME Martin Farrell	COUNTY Delaware	MIN. 4-14-39	MAX. 10-14-45

Robert Mais, a member of the Bailey brothers' bootlegging group, masterminded the kidnapping of nightlife impresario and racketeer William Weiss. After demanding a $100,000 ransom, the group killed Weiss in late 1934. Martin Farrell (above) and his brother-in-law Frank Wiley, both of whom escaped from Eastern State Penitentiary in July 1934, participated in Mais's plot, which left Weiss dead. In January 1935, Farrell led authorities to the Neshaminy Creek, where Weiss's body—wrapped in blankets and weighed down with irons—was dumped. Both Farrell and Wiley were executed for their roles in Weiss's murder; they died minutes apart in Pennsylvania's electric chair on December 2, 1935. (Eastern State Penitentiary Historic Site.)

Irving Wexler, known as "Waxey Gordon," was a prolific pickpocket before rising in the ranks of bootlegging and gambling in Prohibition-era New York City. Before his ascent to the upper echelons of mob kingpin Arnold Rothstein's inner circle, Gordon served time in Philadelphia for his crimes as a sneak thief. Wexler (left) is pictured here with two bodyguards. During Prohibition, Gordon tried to penetrate Mickey Duffy and Max "Boo Boo" Hoff's bootlegging territory. (Library of Congress.)

While it has been assumed that the New York Police Department took this mug shot, Benjamin "Bugsy" Siegel was actually arrested in Philadelphia in April 1928 for being a suspicious character. Although he told the authorities that he was in the auto livery business, he and Meyer Lansky were running a bootlegging gang in New York City at the time. This is his earliest known arrest photograph. (John Binder Collection.)

Philadelphia police kept tabs on organized criminal gangs up and down the Eastern Seaboard, keeping mug shots and lineup shots in their photograph files. This 1934 New York City lineup features a young Frank "Skyball" Scibelli (above, far right), who enjoyed a long career as a mobster in western Massachusetts. New York police wrote that Scibelli and his crew were "Hi Jackers" (below). (Both, Philadelphia City Archives.)

```
            Group #1
New York Group   (Left to Right)
#1 Fred Ferraro       B125376
#2 James Reed         B77165
#3 Frank Massa        B109611
#4 Reggie Colton      B125370
#5 Frank Scibelli     B125371
```

Hi. Jackers

Three

BLOODY ANGLES
TURF WARS AND GANG FIGHTS

NAME				NO.				FORM P12 9-2-35 1300
AGE 48 YEARS	DATE OF BIRTH 6-16-1891				NATIVITY Messina, Sicily, Italy		SEX Male	

RESIDENT IN U.S. 20 YEARS · DATE AND PLACE OF FIRST PAPERS { None · DATE AND PLACE OF NATURALIZATION None

COMPLEXION Med. Dark · EYES Dk Chestnut · HAIR Dk Chestnut · FOOT · BUILD Medium

STATURE 5 FT. 5-3/4 IN. · WEIGHT 178 · INDUSTRIAL RELATIONS

OCCUPATION Live Stock Dealer · WORKING WHEN ARRESTED · HOW LONG BEFORE, IF NOT

PARENTAL AT 16 YEARS FATHER · MOTHER · AGE ON LEAVING HOME { · YEARS

EDUCATIONAL: READS AND WRITES Yes · SCHOOL, PUBLIC OR PAROCHIAL { 4 G YEARS · PRIVATE SCHOOL { YEARS · COLLEGE YEARS · AGE ON LEAVING HOME { · YEARS

HABITS: Moderate · ASSOCIATES: Ordinary · RELIGION: Christian Science SMOKE: · CHEW:

ATTRIBUTE CRIME TO DRINK: · PROFANITY: · CONJUGAL RELATIONS: Single

CHILDREN: · LIVING WITH WIFE OR HUSBAND: · CASH: 73 DOLLARS 28 CENTS

PROPERTY: None

MARKS AND SCARS Faint obl scar on fold l. wrist rear; obl scar on forehead above head r. eyebrow; obl scar in head r. eyebrow; Round depressed scar on r. cheek.

BRIEF HISTORY OF CRIME: Attempted to escape from W.S.P., Pittsburgh, Pa., which resulted in the death of two guards.

COLOR: White · COUNTY: Allegheny · TERM: 187, June, 1924 19

CRIME Murder - Voluntary Manslaughter · JUDGE: Evans

SENTENCE: MIN: 8 YRS. 3 MOS. 11 days · MAX: 20 YRS. MOS. · FINE: 6¢

REMARKS: Plea - Convicted

DATE OF SENTENCE 6-9-24 begins 1-15-40 19 · DATE RECEIVED Re-entered 2-2-40 19

NAME SALVATORE BATTAGLIA (RN) · ALIASES by Tech. Trans. from W.S.P. Emanuele, Salvatore Battoglia, Malfa

ADDITIONAL TIME TO BE SERVED

NO. OF CONVICTIONS: YEARS MONTHS DAYS TIME

NO. D-4631 · NAME SALVATORE BATTAGLIA · COUNTY Allegheny · P 1-15-50 MIN 4-26-48 1-15-60 MAX 4-25-68

EASTERN STATE PENITENTIARY, PA. D-4631 2 2 40

In the early 1920s, Salvatore "Battleaxe" Battaglia was convicted of killing a police officer in a South Philadelphia gambling den operated by underworld figure John Scopoletti. Battaglia was sentenced to Eastern State Penitentiary. Michael Falcone, arrested along with Battaglia, later became an associate of the Lanzetti brothers' gang. (Eastern State Penitentiary Historic Site, gift of John P. Farley, Mary B. Maiden, James J. Farley, Kate Farley, and Bernard C. Farley.)

Salvatore Battaglia, classified by prison administrators as "an agitator among the Italian Element," was transferred to Western State Penitentiary in Pittsburgh in 1923 in the midst of a grand jury investigation into Eastern State Penitentiary. The following year, when he participated in an inmate uprising that left two prison guards dead, his sentence was extended, and he was sent back to Eastern State. Battaglia's aggressive behavior may have stemmed from personal tragedy; both of his parents and eight of his siblings died in a volcanic eruption in Italy in 1908. The state commuted his sentence in 1948 and released him in 1949, upon the condition that he be deported to Italy. (Both, Eastern State Penitentiary Historic Site, gift of Eastern's friends at CAMA-PA.)

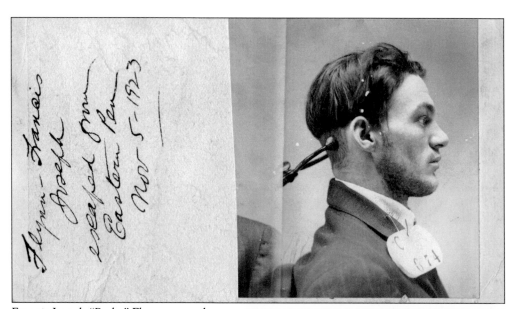

Francis Joseph "Porky" Flynn escaped from Eastern State Penitentiary in November 1923, in the second of two high-profile jailbreaks that disrupted the prison's operations that year. Flynn escaped with three others, and a fifth inmate was shot dead just steps from freedom. The 1920s saw much upheaval among the inmates of Eastern State, with 1923 as a particularly rambunctious year. In May, a grand jury investigation released a report detailing an era of "self-rule" among the inmates, who trafficked in narcotics, bootleg liquor, and prostitution within the prison walls. An inmate gang dubbed "the Four Horsemen" orchestrated many of the illicit exchanges. Salvatore "Battleaxe" Battaglia, whom prison administrators had pinpointed as "an agitator" among the prison's Italian population, was identified by a newspaper as "a close friend of the notorious prison clique." (Both, Special Collections Research Center, Temple University Libraries.)

BUREAU OF POLICE
PHILADELPHIA, PA.

William F. Pius
William Lanzetta
31   5 ft. 6
      136   Sldr.
Black
Chest.   comp Dark
Phila
       Shoe Worker
Arrest 5-7-39
       Susp. Character
icer
g.

Named for Catholic popes, Leo, Pius, Willie (above), Ignatius, Lucian, and Teo Lanzetti controlled numbers running, liquor bootlegging, and narcotics trafficking in South Philadelphia. Perhaps because of their sheer numbers, the Lanzetti brothers—called "Philadelphia's First Family of Crime"—had remarkable staying power. They were implicated or questioned in at least 15 murders between 1924 and 1939. In 1933 alone, five Lanzetti brothers were arrested a total of 63 times. The eldest Lanzetti brother, Leo, was killed in 1925, apparently as retribution for the murder of rival bootlegger Joseph Bruno. After Pius died in 1936, Willie was the third Lanzetti to be killed. Willie's body was found in a burlap sack in Wynnewood, Pennsylvania, in July 1939. News reports speculated that he was killed as retribution for the May 1939 slaying of gangster Danny Day Del Giorno. (Both, John Binder Collection.)

On New Year's Eve 1936, Pius Lanzetti was killed at Joe Grimm's luncheonette near the corner of Eighth and Fitzwater Streets in South Philadelphia (above). Lanzetti was drinking a soda when three armed men marched into the sandwich shop and shot him. Lanzetti had been arrested 19 times over the course of the 1920s and 1930s, in addition to being held briefly as a suspect in the murder of Mickey Duffy in 1931. (Anne Margaret Anderson.)

NAME OF PRISONER	DATE	CAUSING THE DEATH OF	HOW DISPOSED OF
Irwin King	8 18 25	James Quinn	12/4/25 10 to 20 Years E.P.
George W Orr	8 18 25	Nellie Orr	12/3/25 10 to 20 Years E.P.
Gaether Bruce	8 28 25	Charles Bates	11/9/25 Discharged at Court
James Leonard	9 1 25	Elizabeth Leonard	12/4/25 2 to 4 Years E.P.
Alberta Morgan	9 8 25	Annie Freeman	10/9/25 Discharged at court
Ignatius Lanzetta	9 16 25	Joseph Bruno La Carcio	11/23/25 " " "
Carmine Razzino	9 20 25	Murder	12/11/25 " " "
Porter Atkinson	9 21 25	"	12/22/25 Discharged at court
Michael Mc Nulty			

But one of many Lanzetti arrests, Ignatius was held for the murder of Joseph Bruno La Carcio in September 1925. The court discharged Lanzetti (spelled here as "Lanzetta") two months later. Undoubtedly scared for their lives after nearly two decades of violence, Ignatius and Lucian fled to Detroit with their mother after their brother Willie's murder in 1939. Teo followed later, after his release from Leavenworth Prison. (Philadelphia City Archives.)

NAME OF PRISONER	DATE	CAUSING THE DEATH OF	HOW DISPOSED OF
Joseph Easter	4. 29. 26	Commit & Retain Vol Manslaughter	9/17/26 1 to 2 Years CP
William Juliano	5. 7. 26		Electrocuted 3/7/27 1ST Degree
Harry J Bently	5. 7. 26	Harry M Cooper	Electrocuted 3/7/27 1ST Degree
Frank Doris	5. 7. 26		Electrocuted 3/7/27 1ST Degree
Joseph Curry	5. 7. 26		Electrocuted 3/7/27 1ST Degree
Everett Blair	5. 13. 26	Manslaughter by Auto	5/15/26 Discharged by Cor
Thomas W Lawson	5. 14. 26	William Thompson Lawson	5/14/26 " Count

William "Willie" Juliano, an associate of the Lanzetti brothers, owned the car used in the 1925 killing of Joseph Bruno La Carcio, for which Ignatius Lanzetti was held. Juliano, along with three other Philadelphia gangsters, went to the electric chair in 1927 for the murder of a policeman during an attempted holdup of a bank messenger. (Philadelphia City Archives.)

Louis "Fats" Del Rossi, a longtime Lanzetti associate, was incarcerated with Ignatius Lanzetti and Michael Falcone in a New Jersey prison from 1936 to 1939 under the state's Anti-Gangster Act. The imprisoned men's lawyer argued that the law violated the constitutionally protected right to assemble, stating, "No such law has been placed on the statute books since the Dark Ages." The presiding judge retorted, "Perhaps there have been no such gangs since the Dark Ages." (John Binder Collection.)

3143-10			NO	

27 YEARS DATE OF BIRTH December 11, 1903 NATIVITY Philadelphia, Pa. SEX Male.

ENT IN U.S. YEARS | TAKEN OUT / FIRST PAPERS { | NATURALIZED | BUILD Med.

LEXION Dark EYES Hazel HAIR Black FOOT 9¼"

IRE 5 FT. 3-1/8 IN. WEIGHT 163 INDUSTRIAL RELATIONS Unapptrd.

PATION Barber. WORKING WHEN ARRESTED Yes. HOW LONG BEFORE, IF NOT

NTAL AT 16 YEARS FATHER Living MOTHER Living AGE ON LEAVING HOME { 18 YEARS

ATIONAL: READS AND WRITES Yes PUBLIC SCHOOL { 8-G 2 yrs HS YEARS PRIVATE SCHOOL { YEARS AGE ON LEAVING { 15 YEARS

S: Abstainer ASSOCIATES: Ordinary RELIGION: Catholic SMOKE: No CHEW: No

BUTE CRIME TO DRINK: No PROFANITY: Yes CONJUGAL RELATIONS: Married.

REN: None. LIVING WITH WIFE OR HUSBAND: Yes. CASH: 31 DOLLARS 18 CEN

ERTY: None.

S AND SCARS Ft obl scar on 2nd PH left mid finger - Obl scar on 1st PH right ind finger - Face rough - Hair thin on top.

COLOR: WHITE COUNTY: Philadelphia TERM: 462 September, 1929. 19

CRIME Murder 1st Degree.

SENTENCE: MIN. ~~LIFE~~ 3 YRS. 3 MOS. MAX. 20 ~~LIFE~~ YRS. MONTHS

FINE: $None. REMARKS: Accomp C 7467- 6797 JUDGE: Gordon, Jr.

DATE OF SENTENCE 12-5-30 (Death) 10-21-31 Commutted DATE RECEIVED October 31, 1931. 19

NAME DANNY DAY DEL GIORNO ALIASES Daniel Michael Del Giorno - Danny Daniels - Danny Day.

NO. OF CONVICTIONS: 3

ADDITIONAL TIME TO BE SERVED

	YEARS	MONTHS	DAYS	TIME

| O. C 7477 | NAME DANNY DAY DEL GIORNO | COUNTY Philadelphia | MIN. LIFE 1-21-35 | MAX. LIFE 10-21-51 |

Danny Day Del Giorno, referred to as "Danny Day" by the media, and his accomplices Frank Del Vaccio and Anthony Piccarelli were convicted and sentenced to Eastern State Penitentiary for the murder of Samuel Jacobs in July 1929. Day's death sentence was commuted to life in prison, but he only served eight years. Eastern State's Catholic chaplain, Fr. Bernard Farley, agreed to be Day's sponsor when Day was paroled in July 1938. Within a year of his release from prison, Day was shot and killed while driving, and his murder was never solved. Newspapers reported that Day's death was due to a gangland feud over numbers rackets and the white slavery trade (prostitution). Willie Lanzetti, of the infamous gang of brothers, was slain two months later, causing speculation that he died as revenge for Day's death. (Eastern State Penitentiary Historic Site.)

Like many of his gangland associates, Danny Day Del Giorno lived in a row home in South Philadelphia. While incarcerated at Eastern State Penitentiary, he gave this address (the house with the white door) on Bainbridge Street as his permanent home. According to the United Press, Danny Day, as the media called him, had shunned the rackets and was planning to leave Philadelphia to start anew when he was killed in 1939. (Anne Margaret Anderson.)

NAME   NO.

ACME 12149-10

AGE 42 YEARS   DATE OF BIRTH June 4, 1889   NATIVITY Philadelphia, Penna.   SEX Male.

RESIDENT IN U.S. YEARS   TAKEN OUT / FIRST PAPERS (NATURALIZED   BUILD Med.

COMPLEXION Med Dark   EYES   Lt Slate Blue   HAIR Grey   FOOT 9"

STATURE 5 FT. 2½ IN.   WEIGHT 162   INDUSTRIAL RELATIONS Unapptrd.

OCCUPATION Tailor's helper.   WORKING WHEN ARRESTED No   HOW LONG BEFORE, IF NOT 5 months.

PARENTAL AT 16 YEARS FATHER Living   MOTHER Living   AGE ON LEAVING HOME 17 YEARS

EDUCATIONAL: READS AND WRITES Imperf.   PUBLIC SCHOOL (YEARS   PRIVATE SCHOOL (YEARS   AGE ON LEAVING never went. YEARS

HABITS: Moderate   ASSOCIATES: Ordinary   RELIGION: Catholic   SMOKE: Yes   CHEW: No

ATTRIBUTE CRIME TO DRINK: No   PROFANITY: Yes   CONJUGAL RELATIONS: Married.

CHILDREN: None.   LIVING WITH WIFE OR HUSBAND: CASH: 57 DOLLARS 21 CENTS

PROPERTY: 1 U.S.Service Button.

MARKS AND SCARS Ft obl scar on 1st jnt left ind finger - Obl scar on 1st jnt right ind finger - Hor scar on back of neck

COLOR: WHITE   COUNTY: Philadelphia   TERM: 463 September, 1929.

CRIME Murder 1st Degree.

SENTENCE: MIN. LIFE 7 YRS.   MOS. MAX. LIFE; YRS. 23 yrs, 5 mos.   MONTHS

FINE: $ REMARKS: Accomp C 7477 - 6797   JUDGE: Gordon, Jr.

DATE OF SENTENCE 12-6-29 Death Commutted 10-21-31   DATE RECEIVED October 31, 1931.

NAME FRANK Del VACCIO   ALIASES Del Vacco - Dassio

NO. OF CONVICTIONS: 3   ADDITIONAL TIME TO BE SERVED YEARS MONTHS DAYS TIME

NO.	NAME	COUNTY	MIN.		MAX.	
3 7476	FRANK DEL VACCIO	Philadelphia	LIFE	1-21-38	LIFE;	5-6-53

A tailor's helper, Frank Del Vaccio also received a death sentence for the murder of Samuel Jacobs in 1929. Prison administrators commuted his death sentence and gave him life in prison, eventually trimming his sentence even further. "Shorty Frank" Del Vaccio was paroled on Christmas Eve 1938. (Eastern State Penitentiary Historic Site.)

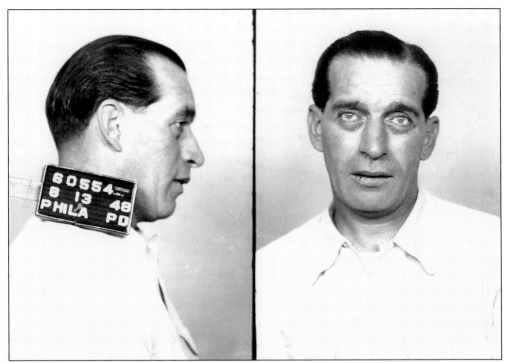

Anthony "Pickles" Piccarelli, implicated in the 1929 murder of Samuel Jacobs, was killed in a drive-by shooting in 1938. The man in this 1948 photograph was also identified as Anthony Piccarelli, though it is unclear if the two men were related. Individual offenders were given one identification number by Philadelphia police, which they then used for each subsequent arrest. This man's number, 60554, indicates that his first arrest was in the 1920s. (John Binder Collection.)

NAME OF PRISONER	DATE	CAUSING THE DEATH OF	HOW DISPOSED OF
James Flori	8.3.29 ✓	Murder	X Electrocuted July 7th 1930 12/13 Electric Chair
Frank Piccolo	8.3 "	"	11-28-30 E. P. 8½ to 17
John Krasowski	8.9 .	Manslaughter	10/5/29 Huntingdon Reform
Frank Del Vacco	8.14.	Samuel Jacobs	X 12/6/19 Electric Chair.
Robert Morton	B 8.14.	Harry L. Hill	9/4/29 Discharged at Court
Anthony Piccirilli	8.14.	Samuel Jacobs	7/30 E. P. 4 to 8 Years
John Shepherd	B 8.19 "	Murder	9/23/29 Discharged at Court
Charles Burwell	B 8.20 "	Viola Campbell	10/17/29 4 Months C. P.

Police homicide records in the 1920s and 1930s reveal a veritable who's who of Philadelphia gangsters. James Flori and Frank Piccolo were indicted for the murder of Pasquale Livoy, while Frank Del Vaccio (spelled here as Del Vacco) and Anthony Piccarelli (spelled here as Piccorilli) were tried for the murder of Samuel Jacobs. All had ties to Salvatore Sabella, boss of the Italian underworld in Philadelphia. (Philadelphia City Archives.)

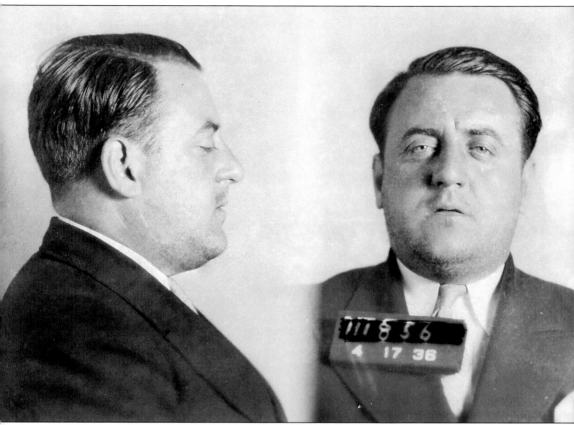

Leonard Nicoletti was a gunman for Salvatore Sabella, who ruled the Italian underworld from 1911 until the late 1920s. Nicoletti worked with fellow gangsters Frank Piccolo and James Flori. The havoc wreaked by gangsters like Nicoletti prompted Mayor Harry Mackey to seek help from the evangelist Billy Sunday. Shortly after the 1928 Special August Grand Jury had been convened to investigate bootlegging and its related violence, Mackey called on Sunday to lead a "great spiritual revival" in Philadelphia. (John Binder Collection.)

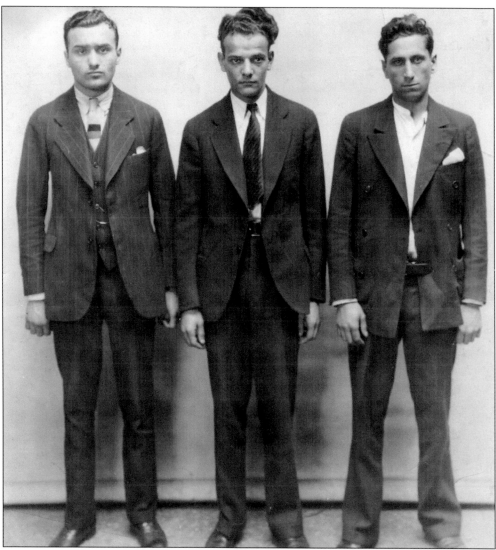

In September 1928, James Flori (right) and Amelio Scarano entered a bottling plant owned by Pasquale Livoy to settle a dispute over alcohol running. Livoy shot at them with a pump gun, taking Scarano's life. A few months later, Flori killed Livoy in retaliation. "Dapper Jimmy," as Flori was known, received the death penalty and was executed in the electric chair in July 1930. Flori and Scarano reputedly belonged to "Scop's Mob," headed by mobster John Scopoletti. Flori is pictured here with Joseph Cusano (left) and Joseph Lucas (center). Cusano was shot to death in 1928 while driving back to Philadelphia from a party in Camden, New Jersey. Newspapers reported that three gunmen in a yellow roadster raced along the Black Horse Pike and shot up Cusano's entourage, which included fellow gangster Danny Day Del Giorno. (Philadelphia City Archives.)

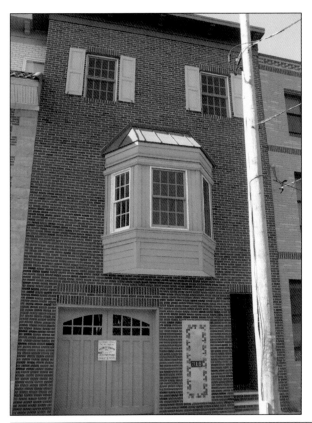

Mobster John Scopoletti ran a gambling den at this address on Passyunk Avenue in South Philadelphia. After a raid here that left a police officer dead, Salvatore Battaglia was convicted of murder and sentenced to Eastern State Penitentiary. (Anne Margaret Anderson.)

In 1926, Saverio Flori, also known as "Sam Flori" or "Sam Einsig," received a sentence of five years and eight months to sixteen years at Eastern State Penitentiary for prostitution charges—pandering and receiving money from pimping. Prison administrators listed a "James Flori," living at a South Philadelphia address, as Sam's brother. (Eastern State Penitentiary Historic Site.)

NAME		NO				
ACHS 12143-10						
AGE 24 YEARS	DATE OF BIRTH 3-6-1902		NATIVITY Naples, Italy		SEX Male	
RESIDENT IN U.S. 17 YEARS	TAKEN OUT FIRST PAPERS Phila- 1920		NATURALIZED U.S.Army		BUILD Slender	
COMPLEXION Dark	EYES Blue		HAIR Dk.Chestnut		FOOT 11"	
STATURE 5 FT. 6½ IN.	WEIGHT 145		INDUSTRIAL RELATIONS Unapprtd			
OCCUPATION Salesman	WORKING WHEN ARRESTED Yes		HOW LONG BEFORE, IF NOT			
PARENTAL AT 16 YEARS FATHER Living	MOTHER Dead		AGE ON LEAVING HOME 20		YEARS	
EDUCATIONAL: READS AND WRITES Yes	PUBLIC SCHOOL 7 YEARS		PRIVATE SCHOOL XX YEARS	AGE ON LEAVING 14 YEARS		
HABITS: Moderate	ASSOCIATES: Ordinary		RELIGION: Catholic	SMOKE: Yes	CHEW: No	
ATTRIBUTE CRIME TO DRINK: No	PROFANITY: Yes		CONJUGAL RELATIONS: Married			
CHILDREN: None	LIVING WITH WIFE OR HUSBAND: No (Prison)		CASH: 0	DOLLARS 68 CENTS		
PROPERTY: 1 Watch & Chain; 1 Knife; 1 Ring; 2 Shirt & 2 Sleeve buttons; 1 Key; 1 Pocket book; 1 Car Token						
MARKS AND SCARS Scar on 1st jnt L index in: Scar running from 2nd to 3rd Ph R index frt: Scar in tail of R ibro:						
Scar under R eye:						

COLOR: White	COUNTY: Schuylkill	TERM: No.655, June	19 26	
CRIME Pandering: Receiving Earnings from one eng aged in Prsostitution: Transportat Etc....				
SENTENCE: MIN. 5 YRS. 8 MOS. MAX. 16 YRS. 0 MONTHS				
FINE: $ 50.00	REMARKS: CONVICTED	JUDGE C.E. BERGER		
DATE OF SENTENCE June 24, 19 26	DATE RECEIVED June 30, 19 26			
NAME Sam Einsig	ALIASES Saverio Flori			

NO. OF CONVICTIONS: 1st	ADDITIONAL TIME TO BE SERVED			
	YEARS 1 MONTHS 3 DAYS back parole.	TIME		

NO.	NAME	COUNTY	MIN.	MAX.		TIME
03466	Sam Einsig	Schuylkill	6-24-34 2-24-32	6-24-42	7-27-42	

John Zukovsky was a rare Prohibition hoodlum. He was taken for a ride by rival gangsters in November 1933 and lived to tell about it, despite being shot in the face, chest, and legs. Those around him, however, were not as lucky. His associate Edward "Cowboy" Wallace died in the same incident, near Bellmawr, New Jersey. Shortly thereafter, their lady friends, Florence Miller and Ethel Marshall, were murdered because they "knew too much." Zukovsky was later sentenced to die in the electric chair for killing a Philadelphia police officer. He received a commutation of his death sentence and was sentenced to life imprisonment at Eastern State Penitentiary, or "E.P." in Philadelphia police shorthand (below). After dodging death a second time and being released early from prison, he finally passed away from a heart ailment in a New Jersey hospital in December 1959. (Above, John Binder Collection; below, Philadelphia City Archives.)

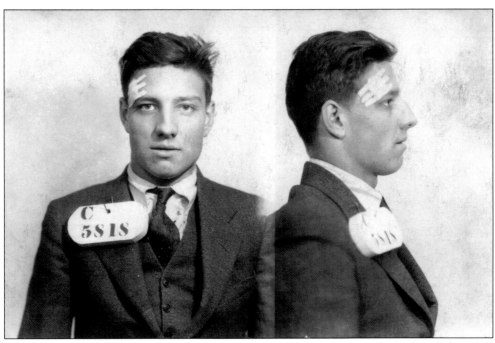

The self-proclaimed "toughest baby" of Philadelphia, William "Blackie" Zupkowski was a fresh-faced 19-year-old when he was sentenced to Eastern State Penitentiary in 1929 for a string of holdups. While incarcerated, his inmate gang rumbled with another inmate gang, and two of his rivals, Max "Chinkie" Rothman and Louis "Fats" Barrish, were stabbed with shanks. This attack in the prison yard was supposedly payback for the death of gangster Eddie Lenny, a former Eastern State inmate who had recently been released from the penitentiary and promptly killed. (Both, Eastern State Penitentiary Historic Site, gift of John P. Farley, Mary B. Maiden, James J. Farley, Kate Farley, and Bernard C. Farley.)

William "Blackie" Zupkowski's life of crime continued after his release from Eastern State Penitentiary. He killed a liquor store clerk during a holdup in Newark, New Jersey, a crime for which he would later be sentenced to death by the electric chair in 1941. (John Binder Collection.)

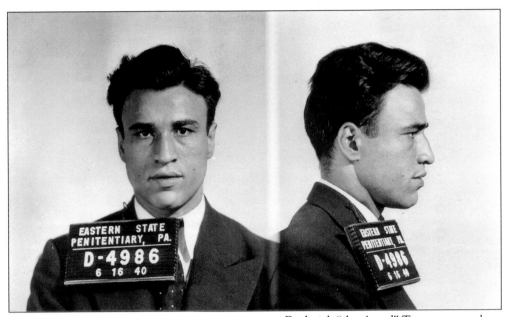

EASTERN STATE PENITENTIARY, PA.
BUREAU OF IDENTIFICATION

No. D-4986.
Name TENUTO, Frederick (RN)
Alias Frank Pinto; Durso Thornberry;
Leonard Durkan; Leonard Durham.
Color WHITE. Age 25 in 1940.
Height 5' 5" Nativity Phila., Pa.
Weight 143 Occupation Butcher.
Build Medium. Hair Black.
Complexion Med.Dark. Eyes Hazel.

Marks and Scars
Imp tat S.J. below fold left elbow
outer; Imp tat ANA right FA outer;
Small brown mole right cheek.

Begins 4--3-40.

Sentenced 6-17-40 / County PHILADELPHIA.
Received 6-17-40. Term 2- to 40 yrs.
Crime MURDER OF THE SECOND DEGREE.
ASSAULT & ROBBERY
F.P.C. (16) O 31 W IOO 19
I 28 W OII 18
Transfd to New E.S.Pen Graterford,Pa.
6-1-42 * E S C A P E D : 9-27-42

2005.011.001

Frederick "the Angel" Tenuto accrued a slew of aliases and a reputation as a hit man during his brief career as a mobster. He escaped from Eastern State Penitentiary and Holmesburg Prison in Philadelphia, both times with famed bank robber and escape artist Willie Sutton. When Sutton was finally nabbed in Brooklyn in 1952 after years of evading the authorities, the man who had alerted the police to his whereabouts, Arnold Schuster, was promptly murdered. It was rumored that New York City mob boss Albert Anastasia ordered the hit on Schuster because he did not approve of tattletales. In addition to being the chief suspect in Schuster's slaying, Tenuto remained on the FBI's Ten Most Wanted list from 1950 to 1964. His later life and whereabouts remain a mystery. (Both, Eastern State Penitentiary Historic Site.)

Photograph taken October 24, 1945   Photograph taken April 3, 1945

Philadelphia was a hub of highly publicized criminal activity, not all of which was gangland related. William "Slick Willie" Sutton was adept at robbing banks and then escaping the prisons in which he was incarcerated. His criminal career spanned the 1920s through the early 1950s. Though Sutton was not connected to the mob, he did escape from two different prisons with gangster Frederick Tenuto. This 1950 FBI WANTED poster of Sutton was released just five days before the FBI compiled its first-ever Ten Most Wanted Fugitives list. Sutton made this list, albeit at No. 11. Tenuto was also on this list, at No. 14. Sutton had been on the lam since his 1947 escape from Holmesburg Prison in Philadelphia. He was captured in Brooklyn in 1952. (Philadelphia City Archives.)

John Avena (center) was boss of Philadelphia's dominant Italian mob from 1927 to 1936. Over Memorial Day weekend of 1927, South Philadelphia gangsters Joey Zanghi and Vincent "Scabby" Cocozza were assassinated. Avena and several associates were picked up and charged with their murders. The court convicted only one man—Luigi Quaranta (right), who was sentenced to Eastern State Penitentiary for the murders. Though sentenced to life, Quaranta received a pardon from the governor after serving just seven years. Philadelphia police identified the man on the left as Joe Guisseppe, though he was more commonly known as "Joe Ida." He served as boss of the Cosa Nostra in Philadelphia from 1946 to 1957. (Philadelphia City Archives.)

Linzo Jones.	5.19.27	William Stevens	Discharged by court
Edward B. Lucey	5.25.27	Goldie Lucey	4/9/28 E.P. for Life
Dorothy Oatler	6.1.27	Commit & Retain for Murder	9/21/27 Discharged by court
John Avena	6.3.27	Murder	7/11/27 Discharged by court
John Scofiletti	6.3.27	"	2/3/28 " " "
Domenick Festa	6.3.27	"	2/8/28 " " "
Salvator Sabello	6.3.27	"	7/11/27 Discharged by court
Luigi Quaranta	6.3.27	"	7/11/28 E.P. for Life
Domenick Pollina	6.3.27	"	7/11/27 Discharged by court
Eileen Thomas	6.3.27	Commit & Retain for Murder	7/1/27 1 to 5 years E.P.

Four out of the six men arrested and tried for the murders of Joey Zanghi and Vincent Cocozza were Sicilian Americans active in the Philadelphia underworld. The most powerful were John Avena and Salvatore Sabella, who preceded Avena as the leader of Philadelphia's dominant Italian mob from approximately 1911 to 1927. (Philadelphia City Archives.)

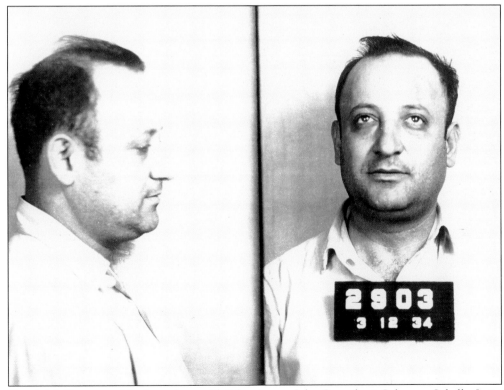

Dominick Festa was picked up, along with John Avena, John Scopoletti, Salvatore Sabella, Luigi Quaranta, and Dominick Pollina, in the 1927 Memorial Day weekend murders of gangsters Joey Zanghi and Vincent Cocozza. Though Festa was not convicted of Zanghi and Cocozza's murders, he remained on the police's radar, as this 1934 arrest shows. (John Binder Collection.)

In 1936, John Avena and his bodyguard Martin Feldstein were killed in a drive-by shooting on a South Philadelphia street corner that had come to be known as the "Bloody Angle." Many gangland incidents had occurred at Passyunk and Washington Avenues, but none were as shocking or misunderstood as the murders of Avena and Feldstein. Avena was the reigning boss of the Philadelphia mob, though newspapers covering his death reported that he was a mere underling of the Lanzetti brothers. Today, the "Bloody Angle" is home to an auto body shop, a hair salon, and a cell phone store, betraying little sign of its dark, storied past. (Anne Margaret Anderson.)

Michael Montanaro was shot and seriously wounded by a detective while emerging from a Philadelphia subway entrance in September 1937. Police captain James Ryan described Montanaro as "one of the biggest of the remaining Philadelphia gangsters." Montanaro was wanted for questioning in the deaths of Pius Lanzetti, John Avena, and Martin Feldstein. (John Binder Collection.)

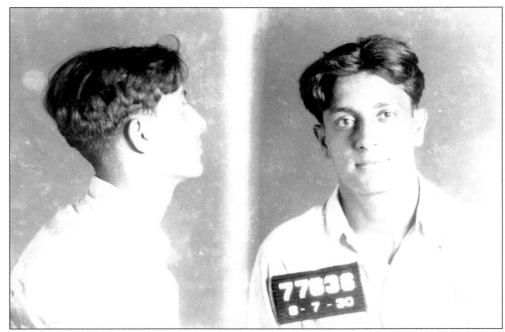

After the murder of underworld figure Pius Lanzetti on New Year's Eve 1936, police looked with renewed interest for Peter Gallo, pictured above and below from two different 1930 mug shots. The fresh-faced Gallo had gone missing since the murder of John Avena, who had been mowed down by shotguns in August 1936. Gallo and John Focoso were the primary suspects in Avena's slaying, though they were never heard from again. The media tied Gallo, Focoso, and Avena to the notorious Lanzetti brothers, and news reports speculated that their respective disappearances and demise stemmed from their status as perceived threats to the Lanzetti empire. (Both, John Binder Collection.)

John Focoso was picked up by the police for a variety of minor offenses from 1929 to 1932, before gaining widespread notoriety as one of the alleged killers, along with Peter Gallo, of John Avena. This photograph was taken when Focoso was arrested for false pretenses and conspiracy. (John Binder Collection.)

After Avena's death, Focoso permanently disappeared from Philadelphia gangland to escape underworld vengeance. This FBI WANTED poster, which lists his arrest record, was issued based on his unlawful flight to avoid prosecution for the Avena murder. (John Binder Collection.)

Many gangland slayings, including the hits on Joey Zanghi, Vincent Cocozza, John Avena, Martin Feldstein, and Pius Lanzetti, took place in and around South Philadelphia's Italian Market neighborhood, which contained both vibrant commerce and searing poverty. The economic activity near Ninth and Montrose Streets (above) coexisted alongside slum-like living conditions, providing South Philadelphia residents with a mix of opportunities and limitations. (Anne Margaret Anderson.)

Four

QUAKER CITY SYNDICATE
THE "NIG ROSEN" MOB

Harry Stromberg, also known as "Nig Rosen," and four of his top men were arrested in Camden, New Jersey, on January 5, 1937, shortly after the murder of Philadelphia gangster Pius Lanzetti. Pictured with Rosen (center) are, from left to right, Pasquale Massi, Raymond Boyne, Phil Di Pietro, and Marco Reginelli. The ethnic mix in this picture illustrates the makeup of the Rosen mob, which included Jews, Italians, and other nationalities. (John Binder Collection.)

Marco Reginelli, known as "the Little Man" or "the Little Guy" due to his diminutive stature at less than five foot three, was a prominent associate of Rosen's who became a major figure in Italian gangdom in Philadelphia. He was the underboss to Joe Ida, the kingpin of the Italian underworld from 1946 to his death in 1956, which made him the de facto gang leader because Ida was essentially an absentee boss. (John Binder Collection.)

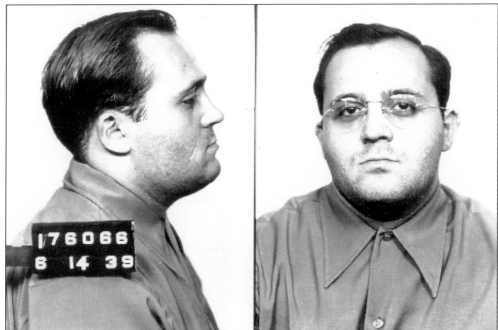

Nathan Stromberg, alias "Nussie Rosen," was the brother of "Nig Rosen." Never an especially high-ranking member of the Rosen gang, he eventually ran the gambling operations in Chester, Pennsylvania. Not surprisingly, his arrest in 1939 was for gambling. (John Binder Collection.)

Public Enemies of New York City

The New York City police labeled the hoodlums in this lineup photograph as "Public Enemies of New York City." They are, from left to right, Harry "Nig Rosen" Stromberg, Benjamin "Bugsy" Siegel, Harry Teitelbaum, Harry Greenberg, and Louis "Lepke" Buchalter. These men were part of a larger group arrested at the Hotel Franconia after the famous 1931 conference in which New York's Jewish gangsters agreed to join the new order created by Lucky Luciano following the slaying of Salvatore Maranzano. Rosen, who had close ties to Buchalter, Siegel, and Meyer Lansky, set up shop in Philadelphia around 1930. Rosen's criminal record stretched back to 1915. Among his charges were juvenile delinquency, robbery, violating Prohibition, assault and battery, and running an illegal lottery. Rosen's mob worked closely with Philadelphia's Italian gang bosses for years, including the post-Prohibition years, when Rosen strategized with prominent Italian gangster John Avena about moving from bootlegging to bookmaking. (John Binder Collection.)

Max "Chinkie" Rothman (right) just barely survived a prison yard shanking at Eastern State Penitentiary, perpetrated by William "Blackie" Zupkowski in 1929. Soon after the stabbing, prison officials transferred Rothman to Western State Penitentiary in Pittsburgh, probably to diffuse tensions among rival inmate gangs. Rothman later gained notoriety as a strong-arm man for mob boss "Nig Rosen." A 1950s federal investigation into organized crime in interstate commerce, commonly known as the Kefauver investigation, reported that Rothman was rumored to be the killer of big-time gangster Benjamin "Bugsy" Siegel, thus solidifying Rothman's reputation as an enforcer. Max "Willie" Weisberg, Rosen's chief lieutenant, is seen on the left. (John Binder Collection.)

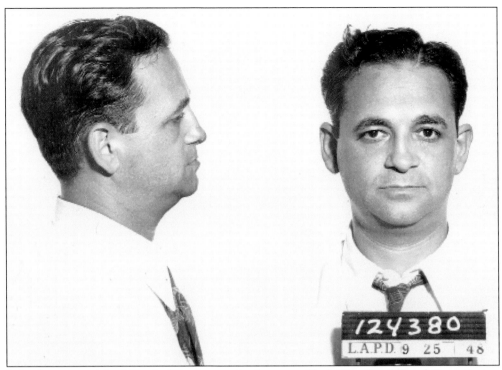

In his later years, Max "Chinkie" Rothman, also known as "Jack Silver" and "Frank Rosso," was a top enforcer for "Nig Rosen." Underworld rumor credited him with being involved in the murder of Benjamin "Bugsy" Siegel in Los Angeles in 1947, and he was, in fact, frequently in Las Vegas and Los Angeles around that time. Rothman was arrested for vagrancy, larceny, arson, assault and battery, and armed robbery before 1951. (Both, John Binder Collection.)

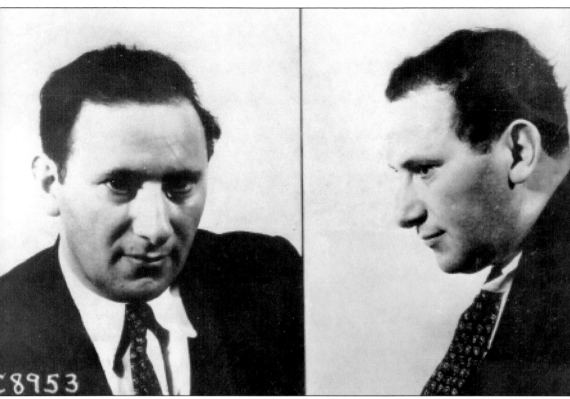

The early-1950s Kefauver investigation listed a number of familiar Philadelphia underworld names. Abe Minker was grilled during the investigation but refused to admit he had any connection to Philadelphia organized crime figures like "Nig Rosen." At the time of the investigation, Minker was an important figure in gambling in Reading, Pennsylvania. When Minker was asked repeatedly by associate counsel Downey Rice to reveal his mob connections, he refused to answer, stating that he did not want to implicate himself in illegal activity. Minker was unwilling to discuss his association with Samuel "Cappy" Hoffman and Max "Willie" Weisberg, both high-ranking "Nig Rosen" lieutenants, or Herman "Mugsy" Taylor, a boxing promoter who cozied up to the mob. (John Binder Collection.)

Max "Willie" Weisberg served as chief lieutenant for "Nig Rosen." Operating out of the Sands Hotel in Miami Beach, the "Nig Rosen" crew of gambling gangsters included longtime associates like Weisberg and Max "Chinkie" Rothman. Not only did Rosen's organization have remarkable staying power, its outposts along the Eastern Seaboard—from New York City, to Camden, to Philadelphia, to Miami—proved its power. (John Binder Collection.)

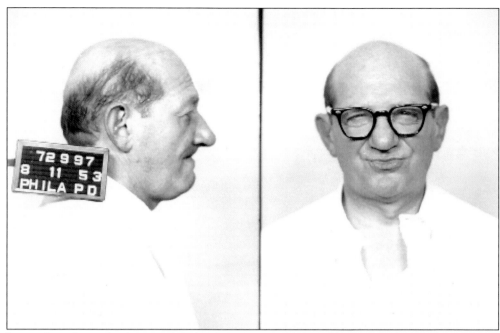

Irving Greenberg, also known as "John Rosen," was another old-time bootlegger who migrated to horse and numbers betting after Prohibition. He was also actively involved in gambling at the Sands Hotel in Miami Beach, a "Nig Rosen" operation that involved a variety of his more prominent gang mates. (John Binder Collection.)

Arrested for larceny, gambling, and homicide at various times during his criminal career, Peter Casella became a trusted associate of Marco Reginelli while he was the underboss of the Philadelphia crime family. Casella was sentenced to 40 years in prison for drug trafficking in 1958 and, after his release, briefly served as the underboss in the early 1980s following the murder of Angelo Bruno. (John Binder Collection.)

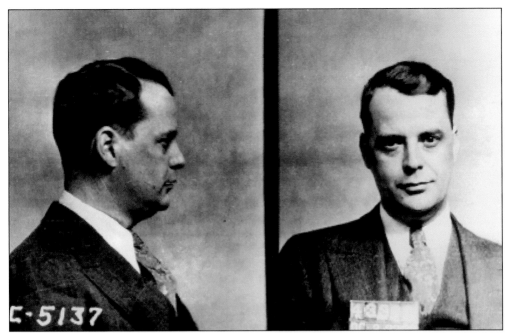

Tommy Leonard, an early business partner of "Nig Rosen" in the numbers racket in Philadelphia, is shown here in a Washington, DC, mug shot taken in 1933, indicating that he might have relocated while maintaining his ties with Rosen. Leonard vanished around 1934, and it was presumed that he was murdered. (John Binder Collection.)

Moe Newman boxed during the late 1920s, participating in more than 20 professional bouts. A lightweight class pugilist, he once fought on the same card as future heavyweight champion Jim Braddock before turning to a life of crime. Newman was suspected of killing white slave (prostitution) kingpin Samuel Reinstein in New York in September 1929. Newman was shot four times that December while standing on a Philadelphia street corner. (John Binder Collection.)

Moe Newman's brother Jack, also known as "Jeff," "Jake," or "John Newman," or "Joseph Schaeffer," started out with Mickey Duffy's gang before becoming a top killer for "Nig Rosen." When he was released from a Minnesota prison in 1948 after serving time with Albert Silverberg for a 1932 mob hit, Newman operated as a bookmaker inside the Ritz-Carlton Hotel in Philadelphia. (John Binder Collection.)

A onetime associate of Mickey Duffy, Albert Silverberg attempted to take control of his bootlegging empire after Duffy's murder. Silverberg's base of operations was in North Philadelphia. Along with Jack Newman and several others, he joined the "Nig Rosen" mob and became a feared executioner. During the 1960s, Silverberg was a common gambler around Philadelphia. (John Binder Collection.)

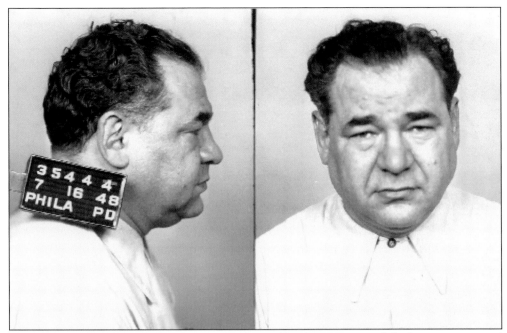

Sad-faced Sam Lit was another Rosen man. A gambler, he ran some of the biggest sports and horse race betting establishments in Philadelphia. Lit was arrested in 1948 for pool selling and, separately, for horse betting at 810 Walnut Street. A police raiding party led by George Richardson, Assistant Superintendent of Detectives, made the latter arrest. (John Binder Collection.)

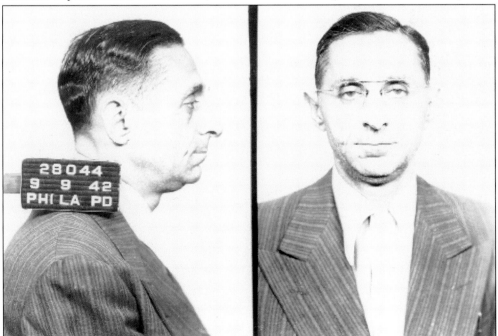

Harry Provan, also known as "Harry Prazansky," got his start in the underworld as a pickpocket and a drug peddler who used his own product. Active in bookmaking and pool selling, he rose to become a gambler in the "Nig Rosen" organization. (John Binder Collection.)

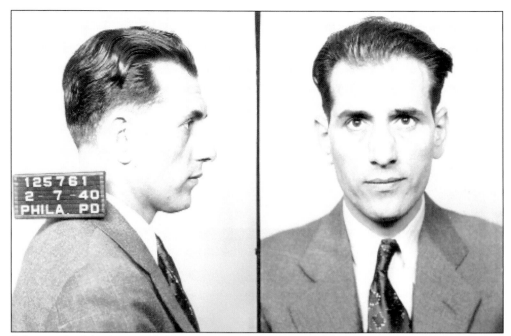

Salvatore Scafidi, the son of old-time gangster Gaetano Scafidi, was convicted of bombing and arson, along with his father and his brother Rocco. This mug shot was taken in 1940 when he registered with police as a known criminal. Later, Salvatore and Rocco Scafidi were members of the Cosa Nostra crime family led by Angelo Bruno, in which their uncle Joseph Scafidi was a capo. (John Binder Collection.)

Pasquale "Patsy" Massi was another "Nig Rosen" gangster during Prohibition who later rose to prominence in Philadelphia gangland. By 1960, he was a capo under Angelo Bruno. Contrary to the Cosa Nostra's "macho" image, Massi was convicted of conspiracy to commit sodomy after he was arrested with a 16-year-old African American boy by a national park ranger in Arkansas in 1967. (John Binder Collection.)

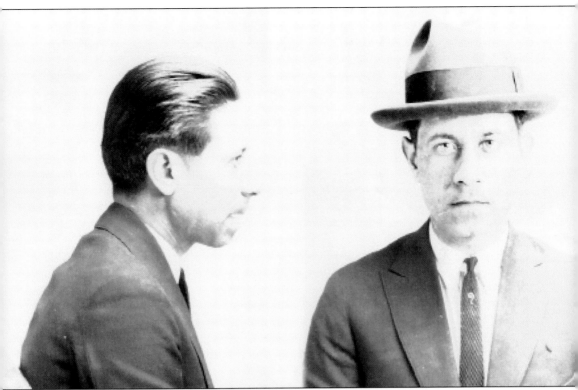

Philadelphia police arrested 25-year-old Phil Di Pietro for being a fugitive in 1923. Police recorded his occupation as "laborer." Di Pietro was later affiliated with "Nig Rosen," arrested alongside the mobster in Camden, New Jersey, soon after the murder of Philadelphia gangster Pius Lanzetti. (John Binder Collection.)

Raymond Boyne (second from left), alias "Johnnie Murphy," was identified as a member of the "Nig Rosen" mob by an early 1950s federal investigation into organized crime. According to the investigation, Boyne worked as a killer and strong-arm man for Rosen. Boyne was a prolific figure in Philadelphia police files; he was photographed in multiple lineup shots, with an array of different characters. (Philadelphia City Archives.)

Raymond Boyne (far right) was at the Jewish Social Club when Samuel E. Grossman and Albert Skale were murdered there in December 1931, reportedly as payback for bootlegger Mickey Duffy's death. In escaping the melee inside, Boyne jumped from the club's roof, onto the building next door, and suffered a broken ankle. He is pictured here with, from left to right, Kenneth Wayland, Frank Morse (alias "Marchese"), and Joseph Keller. (Philadelphia City Archives.)

Felix Bocaccio, known as "Felix Bocchicchio," "John J. Bartlet," "William A. Travers," and by the more appropriate sobriquet "Man of War," was active in gambling and prostitution in the Philadelphia underworld. In the mid-1940s, he became the manager of Jersey Joe Walcott, until then a moderately successful heavyweight fighter. Learning the boxing game as he went along, Bocaccio took Walcott all the way to the heavyweight title. (John Binder Collection.)

Vincent "the Sheik" Amato, also known as "James Amato," was arrested for murder in Philadelphia in 1929 and again in Pottsville, Pennsylvania, in 1938. Standing almost six feet tall and weighing 174 pounds, he was fairly large for a Prohibition-era hoodlum of Italian birth, since many of them suffered from the poor nutrition that was common in Southern Italy in the early 1900s. (John Binder Collection.)

On August 9, 1932, Frank Matteo (left), also known as "Matto," "Mattio," and "Frankie Mendell," was arrested with Harry Passen (center) and Joseph "Sharkey" Saia (right) for robbery, one of the few crimes he probably did not commit. From 1926 to 1936, Matteo was arrested 22 times for offenses including liquor possession, assault and battery, running a house of prostitution, being a suspicious character, and homicide. In the 1940s, he was arrested for gambling, which is consistent with the shift in his activities over time toward illegal games of chance. Frank Matteo and his various brothers were part of the original "Nig Rosen" mob and were later among the most powerful Italian gangsters in Philadelphia, working first under Marco Reginelli and then Angelo Bruno. (John Binder Collection.)

Harry Passen's bullet-ridden body was found in the woods near Williamstown, New Jersey, in 1944. According to investigators' reports, Passen had been shaking down gangsters involved in the numbers or narcotics rackets and was killed while attempting to collect from a blackmail victim. (Both, Philadelphia City Archives.)

CRIMINAL IDENTIFICATION DIVISION
BUREAU OF POLICE
PHILADELPHIA, PENNSYLVANIA

AGE 34	NAME	Harry Passen NO.
WEIGHT 5-6-3/4	ALIAS	Passon, Harris
HEIGHT 155	ADDRESS	2329 S. 8th st
COMP. M Dark		Chauffeur
HAIR Blk		Susp Char
EYES M Mar		Insp. Richardson
BUILD M Slender		

REMARKS: Dead 4-10-44

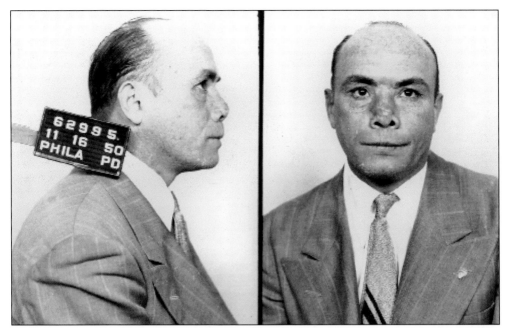

Although physically unimposing at just below five foot five and 135 pounds, Salvatore Matteo, also known as "John Lewis," carried a lot of weight in the underworld. He and his siblings Frank and Nick were the most important of the Matteo clan. This mug shot was taken when Salvatore was arrested as a common gambler in 1950. (John Binder Collection.)

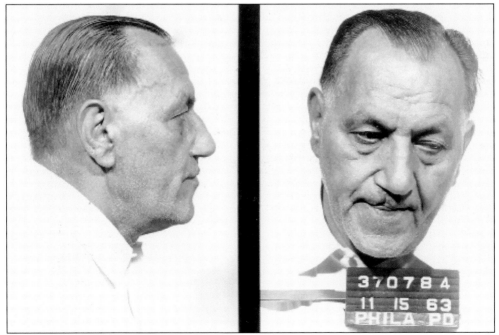

In the 1960s, Nicholas Matteo was still involved in illegal lotteries, sometimes called "pools," which catered heavily to the African American community in the City of Brotherly Love. These games and horse race betting were the cornerstones of the Matteos' post-Prohibition illegal gambling operations. (John Binder Collection.)

Michael Matteo, aliases "Mickie Mendall," "Mike Mandell," "Michael Mattso," and "Henry Green," was one of the less prominent of the Matteos. Nonetheless, from 1925 to 1936, he was booked 21 times on a variety of charges, most of which were related to the family's involvement in alcohol, prostitution, and narcotics. (John Binder Collection.)

This group, arrested in April 1938, exemplifies the gangsters of the period. They were always well dressed and stared without expression at the police camera. From left to right, they are Salvatore Soressa, Joseph LaBarca, Domenic Yanetta, and Frank Lentino. Later, Lentino was an organizer for the largest casino hotel union in Atlantic City and, in 1984, pleaded guilty, along with Atlantic City mayor Michael Matthews, to charges that Matthews had accepted bribes in exchange for helping the Philadelphia mob further its interests in the city. (John Binder Collection.)

Martin Kaufman (left), also known as "Morris Kauffman"; Raymond Boyne (center), also known as "Joseph" or "Johnnie Murphy"; and Lloyd Swartz (right) were arrested together sometime during the 1920s, based on their clothing in this photograph. Boyne was a killer and strong-arm man for "Nig Rosen," in addition to selling whiskey. (John Binder Collection.)

Well dressed but not well intentioned, Moe Newman (left) and Sam Green (right) are shown together in this side-by-side police photograph. Originally from New York City, Newman was a gunman for mobster "Nig Rosen" during Prohibition. He later moved back to New York but continued to work with Rosen. (John Binder Collection.)

Anthony Piccoli, second from the left in this four-man lineup, was arrested with Danny DiLuzzio (left), Frank Bosurgi (second from the right), and Jules Leiberman (right) for armed robbery, most likely during the late 1930s. Unusually, the Philadelphia police took a second standing photograph of just Piccoli and Leiberman related to this arrest. Because it was common for criminals of the era to change a letter or two in their last name when creating an alias to give to the police, Piccoli might very well have been Anthony "Tony Buck" Piccolo, who later served as the boss, and then the consigliere, in Philadelphia's crime family before going to prison. (Both, John Binder Collection.)

Tony Narcisse (left), whose last name was sometimes spelled "Narcissi," was arrested with Philip Kline (right), also known as "Harry Schwartz," on May 4, 1933. A drug addict, Narcisse was an enforcer for "Nig Rosen," and one of his earliest adherents during Prohibition. Later, he was active in gambling outside Philadelphia city limits. (John Binder Collection.)

Five

ARSENIC AND BLACK LACE
POISON-FOR-PROFIT RING

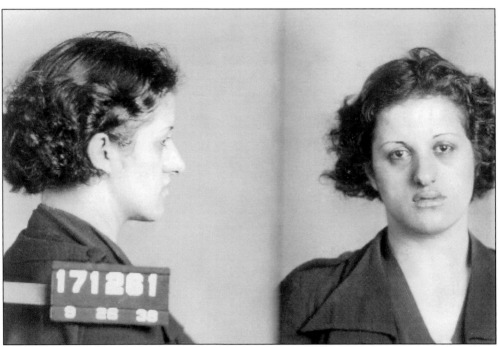

Stella Alfonsi (above) and Herman Petrillo's September 1938 arrests for the attempted murder of Alfonsi's husband could have been misinterpreted as an isolated love triangle turned deadly. Yet these arrests opened the investigative floodgates on a "poison-for-profit" syndicate that dealt in magic potions, witchcraft, insurance fraud, and mass murder. Alfonsi was acquitted of her husband's murder, but the investigation that followed led to 22 murder convictions. (John Binder Collection.)

Herman Petrillo, a father of five, was one of the architects, and casualties, of the Philadelphia arsenic ring. In March 1939, he was sentenced to death for the murder of Ferdinand Alfonsi, whose autopsy revealed that his body was saturated with arsenic. Alfonsi's widow, Stella, received more than $8,000 as the beneficiary of his life insurance policies. Petrillo was convicted of a second murder in May 1940—that of Ralph Caruso. Begging for mercy and proclaiming his innocence, Petrillo died in the electric chair at Rockview, a Pennsylvania state prison, on October 20, 1941. In advance of the poison ring bust, Petrillo was wanted for counterfeiting and bootlegging. He dealt in barber fixtures, according to information supplied when he was booked in May 1937 for arson, though the press much preferred to highlight his past as a spaghetti salesman. (Both, John Binder Collection.)

Herman Petrillo was just another common liquor law violator in June 1931, as shown by this Philadelphia police vice record. Ten years later, Petrillo was executed for his role as an architect in the poison ring murders, his status as a small-time crook elevated to criminal mastermind. With the hope of cashing in on individual life insurance policies, the arsenic ring preyed on the unwitting and the willing. Its ringleaders, including Herman Petrillo, counseled those seeking love potions or healing tinctures, quietly taking out life insurance policies on their beloveds before supplying them with arsenic. The ring also worked with the intentionally malicious, those wanting to dispose of a spouse for their own financial gain. Sometimes, law enforcement and the press did not distinguish between those who had been duped and those who were willing coconspirators. Even today, an aura of mystery hangs over the arsenic ring's cast of characters. (Philadelphia City Archives.)

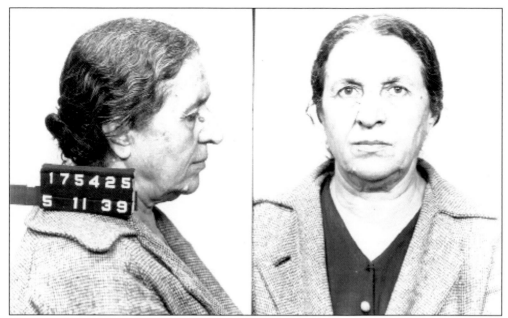

Christine Cerrone, a 68-year-old housewife, took Ralph Caruso in as a boarder in her South Philadelphia home. When Caruso drowned in the Schuylkill River, Herman Petrillo was convicted and executed for his death. Cerrone was a beneficiary for a portion of Caruso's life insurance. She pled guilty to second-degree murder, receiving a sentence of 2 to 20 years in prison. (John Binder Collection.)

A 35-year-old metal worker, Salvatore Sortino pled guilty to assisting Herman Petrillo drown Ralph Caruso in Philadelphia's Schuylkill River in 1934. Police reported that the disabled Caruso was found drowned, clutching his cane in a "death grip," near the Girard Avenue Bridge. Petrillo collected on Caruso's life insurance, netting about $700. Sentenced to life in prison, Sortino served 19 years before being released in 1958. (John Binder Collection.)

Paul Petrillo, Herman's cousin, was labeled the "evil genius" behind the arsenic ring by his nephew John Cacopardo. A tailor by trade, Petrillo was a self-styled "witch doctor" who hawked spiritualism to his superstitious South Philadelphia neighbors while speculating in life insurance. In addition to his conviction for administering poison to Luigi Leviachao (who died in 1932), Petrillo was the first of two individuals, the other being his cousin Herman, executed for his involvement in the arsenic ring. Petrillo died in Pennsylvania's electric chair on March 31, 1941. (Both, John Binder Collection.)

Paul Petrillo's tailor shop was located at this address on South Philadelphia's Passyunk Avenue. Petrillo distributed business cards that read, "Professor P. Patril—Divine Healings, Private Readings." The address he gave for his witch doctor practice was the back door to his tailor shop. It was here that Petrillo and fellow poison ring "architect" Morris Bolber swapped stories about various love potions and spells, forging a business partnership in the early 1930s. As the poison ring investigation grew steam in the late 1930s, their partnership collapsed. Bolber testified against Petrillo, probably to save his own life. During Petrillo's murder trial, he and Bolber participated in an "evil eye" standoff. While the judge and lawyers had their backs turned, Bolber seemingly tried to "work on" Petrillo from the witness stand with an intense stare, prompting Petrillo to point back at him with his first and fourth fingers in an attempt to ward off the evil eye. (Anne Margaret Anderson.)

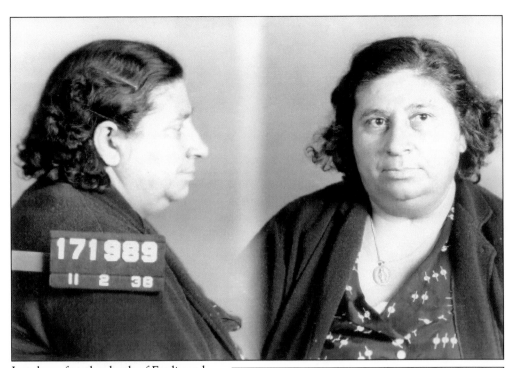

Just days after the death of Ferdinand Alfonsi, Philadelphia detectives exhumed the body of another suspected arsenic death, 17-year-old Philip Ingrao. Large traces of arsenic were found within the corpse, and Carina Favato, Ingrao's stepmother, was promptly arrested. Called the "Philadelphia witch," Favato pled guilty to Philip's murder, as well as the murders of both her common-law husband Charles Ingrao and Guiseppe di Martino, whose bodies were also exhumed and found to be laden with arsenic. She agreed to testify against other syndicate members, triggering a chain of arrests and divulgements. As Favato worked with prosecutors, Philadelphia detectives readjusted their initial estimate of 30 to 70 victims to somewhere around 100 victims. Favato was sentenced to life imprisonment. (Both, John Binder Collection.)

Raffaelle Polselli, described as a former sweetheart of Carina Favato's, pled guilty in late 1939 to first-degree murder in the killings of Charles Ingrao and Guiseppe Di Martino. He received a life sentence, arriving in March 1940 at Philadelphia's Eastern State Penitentiary. Prison administrators noted his role as a "Member of the Arsenic Murder Ring" on his intake card, his accomplice being Herman Petrillo. Polselli died in prison on November 27, 1953. (Above, John Binder Collection; below, Eastern State Penitentiary Historic Site.)

NAME						NO.				
AGE 56 YEARS	DATE OF BIRTH 12-18-1883			NATIVITY Santopedro, Caserta, Italy					SEX Male	
RESIDENT IN U.S. YEARS	DATE AND PLACE OF FIRST PAPERS			DATE AND PLACE OF NATURALIZATION						
COMPLEXION Dark	EYES Dk Chestnut	HAIR Black-Gray		FOOT				BUILD Medium	
STATURE 5 FT. 3 IN.	WEIGHT 122	INDUSTRIAL RELATIONS							
OCCUPATION Laborer	WORKING WHEN ARRESTED		HOW LONG BEFORE, IF NOT						
PARENTAL AT 15 YEARS FATHER	MOTHER	AGE ON LEAVING HOME				YEARS			
EDUCATIONAL: READS AND WRITES Yes	SCHOOL PUBLIC OR PAROCHIAL 5 G	Native YEARS	PRIVATE SCHOOL	YEARS	COLLEGE	YEARS	AGE ON LEAVING HOME		YEARS
HABITS: Moderate	ASSOCIATES: Ordinary	RELIGION: Catholic		SMOKE:		CHEW:			
ATTRIBUTE CRIME TO DRINK:	PROFANITY:		CONJUGAL RELATIONS: Widower					
CHILDREN: Two	LIVING WITH WIFE OR HUSBAND:		CASH: 1		DOLLARS 11	CENTS		
PROPERTY: None								
MARKS AND SCARS Faint obl scar on bridge of nose; Frontal & Tonsorial baldness								

BRIEF HISTORY OF CRIME: Member of the Arsenic Murder Ring - killed two people			
	COLOR: White	COUNTY: Philadelphia	TERM: 732, May, 1939 19
	CRIME Murder First Degree		JUDGE: Rosen
	SENTENCE: MIN: Life YRS. MOS.	MAX: Life YRS. MOS.	FINE: 1¢
	REMARKS: Plea - Convicted Accomplice - Herman Petrillo		
	DATE OF SENTENCE 3-28-40 begins 3-28-40 19	DATE RECEIVED 3-28-40	19
	NAME RAFFAELE POLSELLI (RN)	ALIASES	
	ADDITIONAL TIME TO BE SERVED		
NO. OF CONVICTIONS:	YEARS MONTHS	DAYS	TIME

NO. D-4821	NAME RAFFAELLE POLSELLI	COUNTY Philadelphia	MIN. Life	MAX. Life

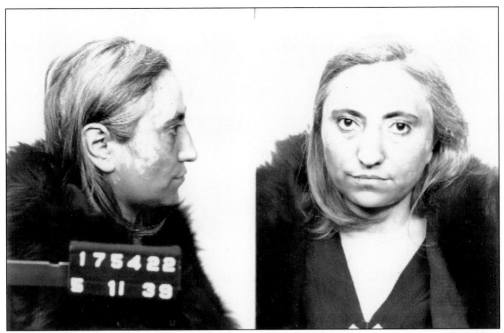

As Herman Petrillo's murder trial went to the jury in late March 1939, presiding judge Harry McDevitt demanded that Susi Di Martino (above) be held without bail in the poisoning death of her husband, Guiseppe. Once the diminutive four-foot-nine Di Martino was led to a jail cell and the jury had convicted Petrillo, Judge McDevitt noted, "It is only by such verdicts . . . that we can ever hope to break the back of this mad quest for money." Susi Di Martino's lover, Emidio Muscelli (below), was also implicated in the death of Guiseppe Di Martino. When detained by police in April 1939, Muscelli collapsed during questioning and had to be revived. Found guilty of first-degree murder, Muscelli was sentenced to life in prison. Di Martino received a sentence of 3 to 20 years in prison. (Both, John Binder Collection.)

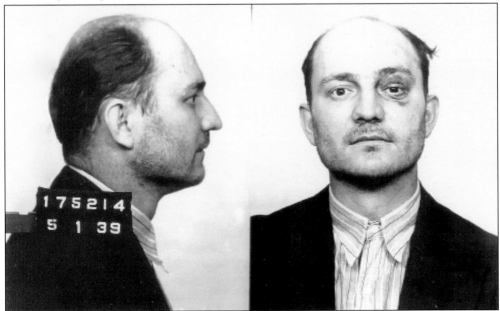

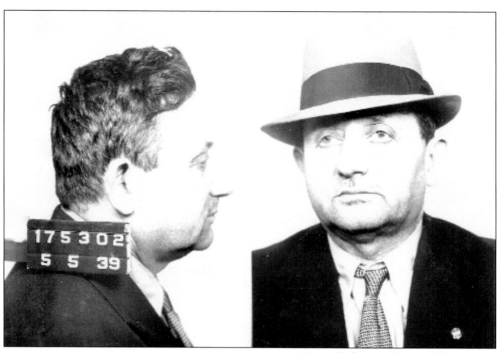

Morris Bolber, nicknamed "Louie the Rabbi," was the last major architect of the poison ring to be arrested. Like Carina Favato, he avoided the death penalty because of his cooperation with investigators. As "executive" of the syndicate, he claimed he knew of 70 poison ring murder victims. While proclaiming his innocence, Bolber noted that he was divulging information "for the benefit of the people of Philadelphia." A self-styled "faith healer," Bolber instructed his clients to do outrageous acts, like hold an egg under one's arm for nine days for good luck or incorporate menstrual blood into a food dish to spice up one's sex life. (Both, John Binder Collection.)

56 YEARS	DATE OF BIRTH 1-3-86		NATIVITY Russia		SEX Male	

<table>
<tr><td>ENT IN U.S. 31 YEARS</td><td>DATE AND PLACE OF FIRST PAPERS 9-13-12-New Brunswick, N.J.</td><td>DATE AND PLACE OF NATURALIZATION 9-13-17 New Brunswick, N.J.</td></tr>
</table>

COMPLEXION Med dark	EYES Trouty	HAIR Black	FOOT	BUILD Medium

| STATURE 5 FT. 5¼ IN. | WEIGHT 159 | INDUSTRIAL RELATIONS | | |

OCCUPATION Store Keeper	WORKING WHEN ARRESTED	HOW LONG BEFORE, IF NOT

| PARENTAL AT 15 YEARS | FATHER living | MOTHER dead | AGE ON LEAVING HOME | YEARS |

| EDUCATIONAL: READS AND WRITES | SCHOOL, PUBLIC OR PAROCHIAL | YEARS | PRIVATE SCHOOL | YEARS | COLLEGE | YEARS | AGE ON LEAVING HOME |

| HABITS: | ASSOCIATES: Ordinary | RELIGION Hebrew | SMOKE: | CHEW: |

| ATTRIBUTE CRIME TO DRINK: | PROFANITY: | CONJUGAL RELATIONS: Married |

| CHILDREN Five | LIVING WITH WIFE OR HUSBAND: Yes | CASH: -40- | DOLLARS -00- |

PROPERTY: 2 Wallets, no value, 2 rings value $7.00

MARKS AND SCARS Arms freckled.

HISTORY OF CRIME: With accomplices was involved in the Arsenic Murder for Insurance Ring.

COLOR: White	COUNTY: Philadelphia	TERM: 889 May 1939

CRIME Murder

JUDGE: McDevitt

| SENTENCE: MIN: LIFE YRS. | MOS. | MAX: LIFE YRS. | MOS. | FINE: 1¢ |

REMARKS: Accomplices: Arsenic Ring

PLEA: Guilty

DATE OF SENTENCE 1-7-42 begins 1-7-42   DATE RECEIVED 1-7-42

NAME Morris Bolber (RN)   ALIASES

| NO. OF CONVICTIONS: | ADDITIONAL TIME TO BE SERVED YEARS | MONTHS | DAYS | TIME |

| NO. D-6210 | NAME MORRIS BOLBER | COUNTY Philadelphia | LIFE MIN. | LIFE MAX. |

Morris Bolber spun an outrageous story about his early life. Born in Russia, Bolber mastered Kabbalah, a Jewish mystical school of thought, as he traveled the world mixing healing tinctures of turpentine, vinegar, alcohol, and horseradish. From 16 to 21 years old, he studied with an ancient witch doctor in China, or so he claimed. At 40, wife and children in tow, he landed in Philadelphia after several years in New York. A failed grocery business behind him, Bolber returned to his supernatural exploits amid his South Philadelphia neighbors, many of them highly superstitious and willing to pay for the love potions and charms he peddled. He was not as invincible as he might have imagined: he pled guilty to the murder of Roman Mandiuk and was sentenced to life imprisonment at Eastern State Penitentiary. He died in prison in 1954. (Eastern State Penitentiary Historic Site.)

DEPARTMENT OF PUBLIC SAFETY
BUREAU OF POLICE
PHILADELPHIA

EDWARD HUBBS
SUPERINTENDENT

DETECTIVE DIVISION

JOHN J. CREEDEN
INSPECTOR OF DETECTIVES

May 25th, 1939

TO: Captain James P. Ryan,

FROM: Commanding Officer, Homicide Division,

SUBJECT: Conduct of ROSE CARINA, alias Tropes,
           while confined in Cell Room, Sixth floor,
           City Hall.

On May 24th, 1939, about 6 P. M., (DST)
while being questioned by Acting Captain James A. Kelly, in
the presence of Detective Anthony Franchetti and Grace
Giovonetti, in Dr. Antrim's room, adjoining the cell room
on the sixth floor, City Hall, Rose Carina, alias Tropes,
fainted. She was carried to her cell by Detective Franchetti,
and while lying on the bed, informed Captain Kelly that she
broke up her glasses, and that she swallowed some of the glass
in the evening of May 23rd, 1939, and some shortly before she
was questioned, which was about 3.30 P. M., May 24th, 1939.
This woman has refused food since arrest on May 18th, 1939.

The Third District Patrol wagon, in charge
of 369 Zubss, took her to the Hahnemann Hospital, where she
was treated by Dr. Maxwell, and detained for further observ-
ation. Her condition is not serious, and she was placed in
Room #642, being further treated and cared for by Dr. Rickert.

369 Woshonopolsky, of the 6th District, was
detailed to her in civilian clothes, and the 6th District was
notified to keep a man detailed there until further orders from
Captain Kelly.

Respectfully submitted,

James A. Kelly
Commanding Homicide Division.

JHMcD

Rose Carina, described by the media as "the kiss of death woman," staged a hunger strike while in jail for her suspected role in the poison ring. After swallowing glass, she was taken to Hahnemann Hospital, where medical personnel force-fed her until she broke her nine-day fast. Described by newspapers as "five times a wife and three times a widow," Carina was eventually acquitted in the murder of her common-law husband Peter Stea. As Carina's nickname indicates, sensationalism surrounded every aspect of the poison ring's news coverage. A May 1939 newspaper headline screamed, "Bodies of Gigantic Poison Ring Victims Pile Up Faster Than Chemists Analyze Them." (John Binder Collection.)

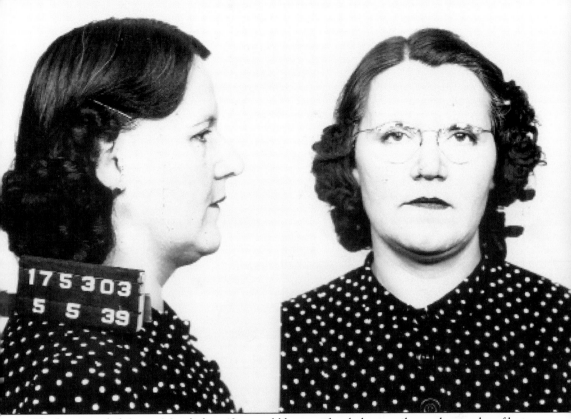

The bespectacled Agnes Mandiuk, a 43-year-old housewife, pled not guilty to the murder of her husband, Roman, a baker. A jury of four women and eight men found her guilty of poisoning Roman to collect on his life insurance, worth $13,000. Though sentenced to life in prison, she eventually received a commutation on Christmas Eve 1954. (John Binder Collection.)

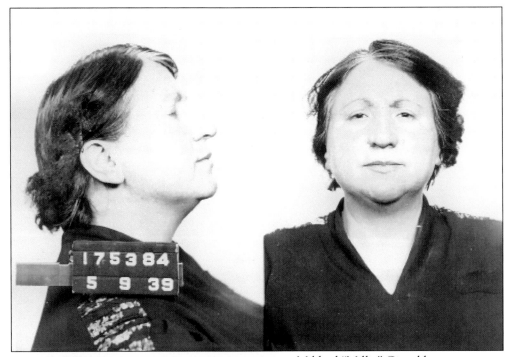

Mildred "Millie" Giacobbe was a storekeeper who lived in this building on South Philadelphia's bustling Passyunk Avenue (left). She was arrested and charged with the murder of her husband, Antonio. While testifying in Paul Petrillo's trial, Morris Bolber claimed that Petrillo had killed Antonio less for the insurance money and more because he was in love with Millie. Though sentenced to life in prison, Giacobbe was released on commutation in March 1956. (Above, John Binder Collection; left, Anne Margaret Anderson.)

			NO.			

47 YEARS DATE OF BIRTH 5-14-93 NATIVITY Italy SEX

NT IN U.S 32 YEARS DATE AND PLACE OF FIRST PAPERS 1911 Phila., Pa. DATE AND PLACE OF NATURALIZATION 1917 Phila. Pa. Court House.

LEXION Med fair EYES Azure blue HAIR Mixed-grey FOOT BUILD Medium

RE 5 FT. 7-1/2 IN. WEIGHT 152 INDUSTRIAL RELATIONS

RATION Presser WORKING WHEN ARRESTED HOW LONG BEFORE, IF NOT

TAL AT 16 YEARS FATHER MOTHER AGE ON LEAVING HOME YEARS

Imperfect ATIONAL: READS AND WRITES SCHOOL, PUBLIC OR PAROCHIAL 2 G Native YEARS PRIVATE SCHOOL YEARS COLLEGE YEARS AGE ON LEAVING HOME YE

S: Moderate ASSOCIATES Ordinary RELIGION None SMOKE CHEW

UTE CRIME TO DRINK: PROFANITY CONJUGAL RELATIONS: Widower

RN Four LIVING WITH WIFE OR HUSBAND: CASH: — DOLLARS .10 CE

TY: None

S AND SCARS Flesh mole below lobe of r. ear; obl scar center of groin.

HISTORY OF CRIME: Gave his wife arsenic which resulted in her death.

COLOR: White COUNTY: Philadelphia TERM: 316 July, 1939 19

CRIME Murder JUDGE: Smith

SENTENCE: MIN: Life YRS. MOS. MAX: Life YRS. MOS. FINE: 1¢

REMARKS Plea - Guilty Accomplices: Providas Machielic - Life David Brandt - #1-1185

DATE OF SENTENCE 10-28-40 begins 6-15-38 19 DATE RECEIVED 10-28-40 19

NAME DOMINICK FRANK CASSETTI (RN) ALIASES

6-7-55 - Letter rec'd from Court giving credit for commitment time. 5894-E P.B.P.

NO. OF CONVICTIONS: ADDITIONAL TIME TO BE SERVED YEARS MONTHS DAYS TIME

NO. D-5325 NAME DOMINICK FRANK CASSETTI COUNTY Philadelphia 5-7-5- 2-1-58 LIFE MAX.

Men also fell victim to the arsenic ring's powerful pressure. The Italian-born Dominick Frank Cassetti testified that two of the lesser "witches," Josephine Sadita and Providenza Micciche, had used witchcraft and "malocchio," or the evil eye, to coerce him into poisoning his wife, Jennie, with arsenic after he sought their help in healing his wife's illness. Sadita and Micciche held séances in Cassetti's candlelit basement, eventually taking a cut of the insurance profits when Mrs. Cassetti died. Casetti served 17.5 years at Eastern State Penitentiary, eventually earning parole in February 1958. (Eastern State Penitentiary Historic Site.)

A typewriter salesman and alleged poison runner, David Brandt was implicated as an accomplice to Dominick Cassetti in the murder of Cassetti's wife, Jennie. When Herman Petrillo, Morris Bolber, and Brandt were questioned together by detectives, each was terrified of being the recipient of the evil eye. The *New York Times* reported the men would frequently interrupt each other with, "Don't you look at me that way; don't you give me the eye." (John Binder Collection.)

31 YEARS	DATE OF BIRTH 8-27-1908	NATIVITY New York City, N.Y.		SEX Male

...NT IN U.S. YEARS	DATE AND PLACE OF FIRST PAPERS	DATE AND PLACE OF NATURALIZATION	

...LEXION Med. Dark   EYES Hazel   HAIR -   ...   Black   FOOT   BUILD Slender

...URE 5 FT. 2-3/4 IN.   WEIGHT 123   INDUSTRIAL RELATIONS

...RATION Salesman   WORKING WHEN ARRESTED   HOW LONG BEFORE, IF NOT

...NTAL AT 16 YEARS   FATHER   MOTHER   AGE ON LEAVING HOME   YEARS

...ATIONAL; READS AND WRITES Yes   SCHOOL, PUBLIC OR PAROCHIAL { 3 U.P. YEARS   PRIVATE SCHOOL   YEARS   COLLEGE   YEARS   AGE ON LEAVING HOME

...TS: Abstainer   ASSOCIATES: Ordinary   RELIGION: Hebrew   SMOKE: CHEW:

...BUTE CRIME TO DRINK: PROFANITY: CONJUGAL RELATIONS: Married

...REN: None   LIVING WITH WIFE OR HUSBAND: Separated   CASH: 82   DOLLARS 08

...ERTY: None

...S AND SCARS   Obl scar above head l. eyebrow; Dimple in chin; Tonsorial & Frontal;

HISTORY OF CRIME: Concealed information of death of two women in Arsenic Murders.

COLOR: White	COUNTY: Philadelphia TERM: 875, June, 1939 / 316, July, 1939 19
CRIME Murder, 2nd Degree (2 Bills)	JUDGE: Bok
SENTENCE: MIN: 2 YRS. MOS.	MAX: 20 / 9 YRS // MOS. FINE: —

REMARKS: Plea - Guilty   Accomplice - Dr. Pearlman (Awaiting Trial) D-5478
DATE OF SENTENCE 12-12-39 begins 5-26-39   19   DATE RECEIVED 12-12-39   19
NAME DAVID BRANDT (RS)   ALIASES

ADDITIONAL TIME TO BE SERVED			
NO. OF CONVICTIONS:	YEARS	MONTHS	DAYS TIME

NO. D-4485   NAME DAVID BRANDT (RS)   COUNTY Philadelphia   5-26-41 MIN.   5-26-56 MAX. 4-26-49

David Brandt entered a not-guilty plea on May 25, 1939, when 29 of the ring's participants were arraigned. Nonetheless, he faced indictment, along with Horace Perlman and Paul Petrillo, for the murder of Jennie Cassetti on June 21, 1939. Brandt eventually pled guilty to second-degree murder, received a sentence of 2 to 20 years at Eastern State Penitentiary, served the minimum, and was paroled on May 26, 1941. (Eastern State Penitentiary Historic Site.)

The arsenic syndicate employed a variety of professionals and gophers: insurance agents, poison providers, undertakers, hit men, and medical professionals. Dr. Horace Perlman was the ring's obstetrician and gynecologist. If a woman sought the "witch doctor" Morris Bolber's help in ending an unwanted pregnancy, he would refer her to Perlman. If Perlman performed an abortion for her, the ring could leverage this secret, threatening her until she agreed to take part in an insurance scheme. Perlman pled guilty to the second-degree murder of Jennie Cassetti. He received a sentence of 10 to 20 years at Eastern State Penitentiary, but he was paroled in November 1948. Former director of public safety Lemuel Schofield served as attorney to Perlman and Paul Petrillo. (Above, John Binder Collection; below, Eastern State Penitentiary Historic Site.)

AGE: 54 YEARS	DATE OF BIRTH 7-4-86	NATIVITY Russia	SEX Male
RESIDENT IN U.S. 47 YEARS	DATE AND PLACE OF FIRST PAPERS (1906 U.S. Dist. Court Phila.	DATE AND PLACE OF NATURALIZATION 1906 U.S. Dist. Court, Phila	
COMPLEXION Dark EYES Grey	HAIR Grey	FOOT	BUILD Slender
STATURE 5 FT. 5-1/4 IN.	WEIGHT 122	INDUSTRIAL RELATIONS	
OCCUPATION Physician	WORKING WHEN ARRESTED	HOW LONG BEFORE, IF NOT	
PARENTAL AT 16 YEARS FATHER	MOTHER	AGE ON LEAVING HOME	YEARS
EDUCATIONAL: READS AND WRITES Yes	SCHOOL, PUBLIC Medical OR PAROCHIAL College YEARS	PRIVATE SCHOOL YEARS	COLLEGE YEARS	AGE ON LEAVING HOME	YEARS
HABITS: Moderate	ASSOCIATES: Ordinary	RELIGION: Hebrew	SMOKES: CHEW:
ATTRIBUTE CRIME TO DRINK:	PROFANITY:	CONJUGAL RELATIONS: Married	
CHILDREN: 3	LIVING WITH WIFE OR HUSBAND: Yes	CASH: 11	DOLLARS 08 CENTS
PROPERTY: 1 Wrist Watch & band, value $5.00; 1 Wallet, no value.			
MARKS AND SCARS Faint irreg rag scar on fold 1 wrist front; chin part bi-lobe; scar of boil on back of neck r of ML			

BRIEF HISTORY OF CRIME: Killed one Jennie Pino by arsenic

COLOR: White	COUNTY: Philadelphia	TERM: 676 June, 1940 19
CRIME Murder		JUDGE: Lewis & Oliver
SENTENCE: MIN: 10 YRS. MOS.	MAX: 20 YRS. MOS.	FINE: 1¢

REMARKS: Plea - Guilty

DATE OF SENTENCE 12-20-40 begins 5-6-39 19   DATE RECEIVED 12-20-40 19

NAME HORACE PERLMAN   ALIASES Horace David Perlman (EN)
Horace D. Perlman

ADDITIONAL TIME TO BE SERVED	
NO. OF CONVICTIONS:	YEARS MONTHS DAYS TIME

NO. D-5443 NAME HORACE PERLMAN   COUNTY Philadelphia   5-6-49 MIN.   5-6-59 MAX.

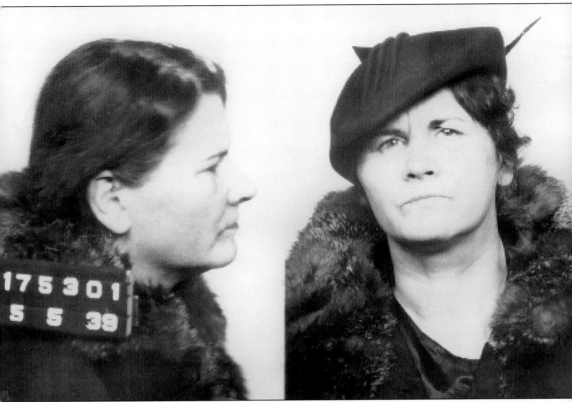

Marie Woloshyn collected $10,600 in insurance on her husband's life, for which she avoided conviction due to a lack of evidence implicating her in his death. When coroner Charles Hersch exhumed Woloshyn's husband's body, he reported that it contained no traces of poison. Investigators believed John Woloshyn's death, by a hit-and-run motorist in January 1936, was actually staged by members of the ring. (John Binder Collection.)

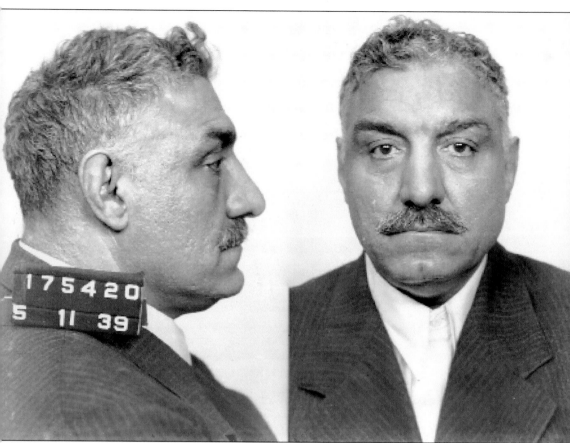

Caesar Valenti was incarcerated in New York's Rikers Island penitentiary for liquor law violations when the poison ring investigation broke open. Investigators brought Valenti to Philadelphia just days before immigration officials planned to deport him to Italy. Considered a key director of the poison ring, Valenti pled guilty to the murder of Charles Ingrao and was sentenced to life in prison. He was also suspected in the death of John Woloshyn. (John Binder Collection.)

In May 1939, newspaper headlines reported breathlessly on the investigation's progress. Philadelphia police were "working 24 hours a day making arrests, exhuming bodies, grilling prisoners, and seeking new suspects and more victims," according to the press. Swept up in the investigation was insurance agent Gaetano Cicinato, who was implicated in killing Joseph Arena and possibly others. Not only did he escape a prison sentence, but he also was never convicted. He went free in June 1939, after spending just one month in custody. (John Binder Collection.)

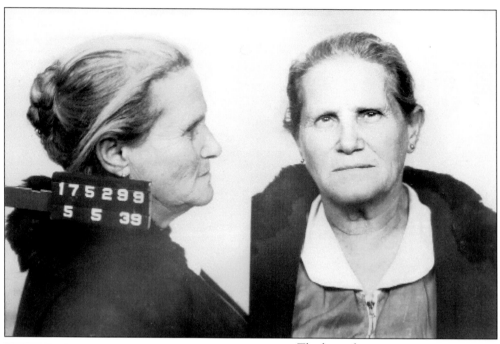

The huge dragnet arresting arsenic widows and their associates continued through the spring of 1939. Chicken dealer Dora Sherman was arrested and accused of conspiring to murder her husband, Abraham, who died in 1936. The Shermans were associates of Morris Bolber, whom they had hired as a faith healer for their disabled grandson. Abraham's death was initially attributed to acute coronary thrombosis, though when the Shermans' association to Bolber was revealed, investigators questioned his official cause of death. (Both, John Binder Collection.)

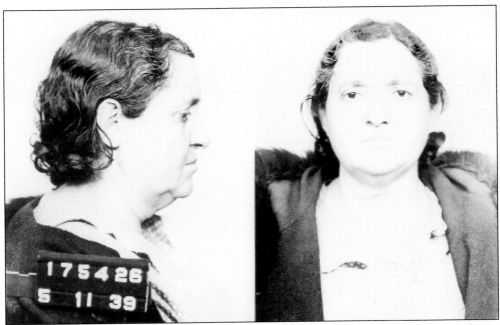

As the poison ring investigation gained steam, Rose Davis Leviachao (above) and Anna Arena (below) were arrested on the same day in May 1939 and held for the deaths of their husbands, both of whom had died years earlier. Leviachao was found guilty of second-degree murder in the poisoning death of her husband, Luigi, who died in 1932. Morris Bolber had furnished arsenic and antimony to Paul Petrillo, who administered a fatal dose to Luigi. Newspapers reporting on Leviachao's case noted with suspicion that she had remarried soon after Luigi's death. Arena, who wore a veil for her mug shot, was implicated in killing her husband, Joseph, who had drowned seven years earlier off the New Jersey coast. She was freed a month after her arrest on jurisdictional issues. (Both, John Binder Collection.)

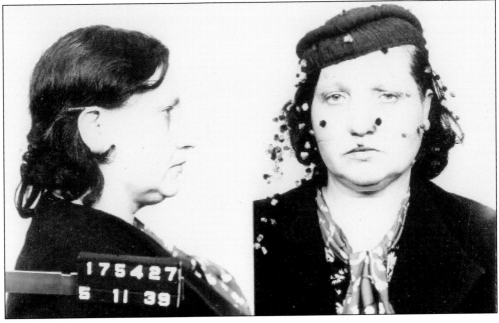

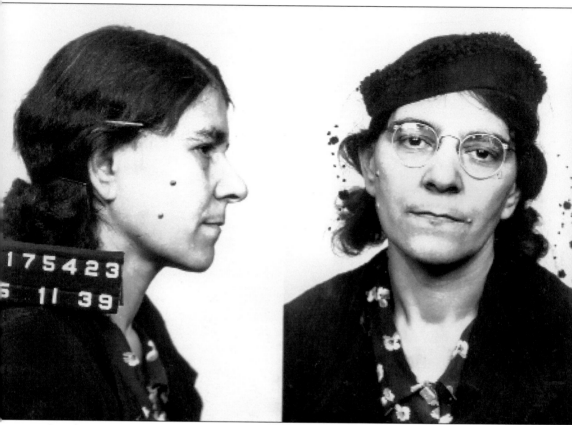

Josephine Romaldo was found guilty of killing her husband, Antonio, a lamplighter. She received a death sentence, one of the few meted out to the poison ring. When sentenced, Romaldo reportedly cried, "I am not guilty, but I am willing to plead guilty for the sake of my children." She claimed that she had only intended to give her husband love potions to rekindle his affections. Her sentence was commuted to life, and she was paroled in December 1958. (John Binder Collection.)

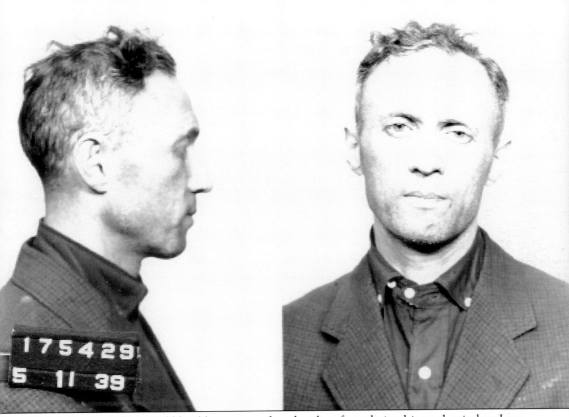

Joseph Swartz, a 40-year-old bookkeeper, was found guilty of murdering his mother-in-law, Lena Winkleman, one of the few female victims of the poison ring. Police captain James Kelly claimed Swartz poisoned Winkleman for the simple reason that they could not "get along." Swartz died in prison in 1940 before he could be sentenced. (John Binder Collection.)

BIBLIOGRAPHY

Allerfeldt, Kristofer. *Crime and the Rise of Modern America: A History from 1865–1941*. New York: Routledge, 2011.

Baldwin, Fred D. "Smedley D. Butler and Prohibition Enforcement in Philadelphia, 1924–1925." *Pennsylvania Magazine of History and Biography* 84 (July 1960): 352–368.

Cooper, George. *Poison Widows: A True Story of Witchcraft, Arsenic, and Murder*. New York: St. Martin's Press, 1999.

Haller, Mark H. "Philadelphia Bootlegging and the Report of the Special August Grand Jury." *Pennsylvania Magazine of History and Biography* 109 (April 1985): 215–233.

———*Life Under Bruno: The Economics of an Organized Crime Family*. Conshohocken, PA: Pennsylvania Crime Commission, 1991.

Morello, Celeste A. *Before Bruno: Book 1 – 1880–1931: The History of the Philadelphia Mafia*. Philadelphia: The Author, 2000.

———*Before Bruno: Book 2 – 1931–1946: The History of the Philadelphia Mafia*. Philadelphia: Jefferies & Manz, Inc., 2001.

———*Before Bruno & How He Became Boss: Book 3 – 1946–1959: The History of the Philadelphia Mafia*. Philadelphia: The Author, 2005.

Pennsylvania Crime Commission. *A Decade of Organized Crime: 1980 Report*. St. Davids, PA: Pennsylvania Crime Commission, 1980.

Potter, Gary W., and Philip Jenkins. *The City and the Syndicate: Organizing Crime in Philadelphia*. Lexington, MA: Ginn Press, 1985.

US Congress, Senate. *Investigation of Organized Crime in Interstate Commerce: Hearings before a Special Committee to Investigate Organized Crime in Interstate Commerce, Part 1: Florida*. Washington, DC: US Government Printing Office, 1950.

———*Investigation of Organized Crime in Interstate Commerce: Hearings before a Special Committee to Investigate Organized Crime in Interstate Commerce, Part 11: Pennsylvania*. Washington, DC: US Government Printing Office, 1951.

———*Investigation of Organized Crime in Interstate Commerce: Hearings before a Special Committee to Investigate Organized Crime in Interstate Commerce, Part 19: Pennsylvania*. Washington, DC: US Government Printing Office, 1951.

Young, Robert James, Jr. "Arsenic and No Lace: The Bizarre Tale of a Philadelphia Murder Ring." *Pennsylvania History* 67 (Summer 2000): 397–414.

INDEX

DISCOVER THOUSANDS OF LOCAL HISTORY BOOKS FEATURING MILLIONS OF VINTAGE IMAGES

Arcadia Publishing, the leading local history publisher in the United States, is committed to making history accessible and meaningful through publishing books that celebrate and preserve the heritage of America's people and places.

Find more books like this at
www.arcadiapublishing.com

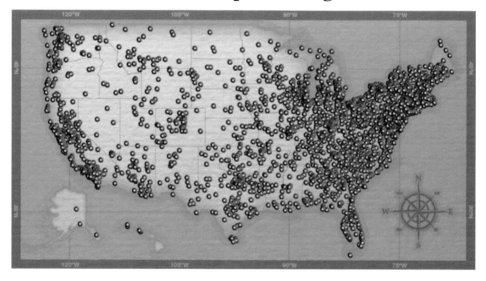

Search for your hometown history, your old stomping grounds, and even your favorite sports team.

Consistent with our mission to preserve history on a local level, this book was printed in South Carolina on American-made paper and manufactured entirely in the United States. Products carrying the accredited Forest Stewardship Council (FSC) label are printed on 100 percent FSC-certified paper.

MADE IN THE USA